Climbing Mt. Whitney

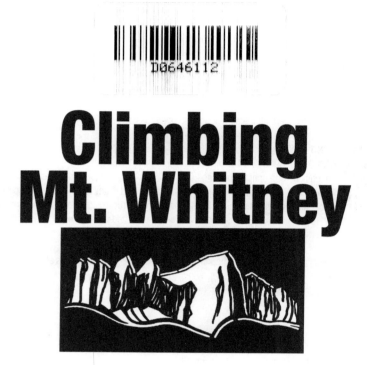

Peter Croft

Wynne Benti

Foreword by Glen Dawson

Member of the East Face first ascent party led by Norman Clyde

Up the East Face

**The Story of the First Ascent, Mt. Whitney's East Face
by Norman Clyde**

**SPOTTED
DOG PRESS**®
BISHOP, CALIFORNIA

Climbing Mt. Whitney

Published exclusively by Spotted Dog Press, Inc., Bishop, California
Spotted Dog Press is a registered trademark of Spotted Dog Press, Inc.

ISBN 1-893343-14-6
ISBN 978-1-893343-14-6
3rd edition, 44th updated printing 2008

If you have comments about this book or others by Spotted Dog Press, please write us at:
Spotted Dog Press
P.O. Box 1721
Bishop CA 93515
800-417-2790
FAX 760-872-1319
store@spotteddogpress.com
Front Cover: East Face of Mt. Whitney by Galen Rowell
Back Cover: The North Fork Approach by Dan Patitucci/Patitucci Photo
Book design, layout, and logo by Wynne Benti

Library of Congress Cataloging-in-Publication Data
Croft, Peter, 1958-
Climbing Mt. Whitney/Peter Croft & Wynne Benti; introduction by Glen Dawson.--
3rd ed.
    p. cm
Rev. ed. of: The Original Climbing Mt. Whitney/Walt Wheelock and Wynne Benti. 1st ed. 1997
Contains an article by Norman Clyde.
Includes bibliographical references and index.
ISBN 1-893343-14-6
    1. Mountaineering--California--Whitney, Mount--Guidebooks. 2.
Hiking--California--Whitney, Mount--Guidebooks. 3. Backpacking--California--Whitney,
Mount--Guidebooks. 4. Whitney, Mount (Calif.)--Guidebooks. I. Benti, Wynne. II. Clyde, Norman, 1885-1972.
III Wheelock, Walt, Original Climbing Mt. Whitney. IV. Title.

GV199.42C22W456 2005
917.94'86--dc22

                                                            2005049991

Printed in the United States of America

Hike and climb at your own risk

Various aspects of hiking, which include climbing mountains, have certain risks and hazards associated with them. Some of these hazards include, but are not limited to: adverse weather conditions, rugged terrain, loose rock, exposed rock, rockfall, falling on rock, equipment failure, stream crossings, insect or snake bites, hypothermia, heat exhaustion, dehydration, mountain sickness or other types of injury which could lead to permanent physical impairment or death.

A book or map is not a substitute for experience, skill, and knowledge of safety procedures. The authors and publisher of this guide make no representations as to the safety of any hiking or driving route described in this guide. Conditions are constantly changing and it is recommended that you contact the supervising federal lands agency or consult available map information to find out about current conditions. The responsibility for your decisions and actions is yours alone.

Acknowledgements

The writers and publisher would like to thank the Mt. Whitney Wilderness Rangers, the Mt. Whitney Wilderness Permit Reservation Office, the Inyo National Forest, Glen Dawson, Marty Lewis, Andy Zdon, and Dr. Charles Houston for their input on this and previous editions.

Galen Rowell and Peter Croft on the summit of Mt. Whitney
PHOTO: Galen Rowell/Mountain Light Gallery

Table of Contents

Foreword

Glen Dawson

Before 1931, climbing in the High Sierra was done without ropes. Firewood was plentiful, no permits were required. It was easier to find places where it was not that difficult to imagine that you were the first to explore. In summit registers there were entries by Walter Starr, Jr. or Norman Clyde and peaks with no sign of prior ascent. There were no cell phones. No one thought about insurance. No special equipment was required.

The object then was to reach a summit by the easiest, safest, fastest route with the least effort. Traverses were made only to climb two or more peaks in one day. Now some climbers look for the most difficult way to climb a summit.

It was Francis Farquhar who first envisioned climbing the East Face of Mt. Whitney. He invited Robert Underhill to write an article about using a rope in climbing for the Sierra Club Bulletin. In 1931, Francis organized a climbing school in the Palisades with Underhill as the instructor and Norman Clyde as a guide. Jules Eichorn and I, both nineteen years old at the time were invited to attend. Thunderbolt Peak was climbed for the first time.

Upon completion of the Palisade School, five of us went south to look at Mt. Whitney. The result, the ascent of August 16, 1931 is well-documented in the climbing books. The 75th anniversary of our first ascent of Whitney's East Face is 2006.

The Palisades Climbing School 1931
Back row: Francis Farquhar, Bestor Robinson, Glen Dawson, Neil Wilson, Lewis Clark
Robert Underhill, Norman Clyde, Jules Eichorn, Elmer Collett PHOTO: Glen Dawson Collection

I am notable only as an historical curiosity or perhaps as a living fossil My career as a rock climber spanned the years 1927 to about 1938. During my lifetime I have been an antiquarian bookseller and publisher but that one event of August 16, 1931 is my footnote in climbing history.

Norman Clyde became a folk legend. Robert Underhill married Miriam O'Brien and together they were a noted climbing and writing team. Jules Eichorn climbed the Cathedral Spires with Richard Leonard and Bestor Robinson, and became the first Yosemite climbing ranger. Jules taught music and took boys on High Sierra trips, hiring Norman Clyde to assist. World War II scattered our rock climbing group across the globe. Richard Leonard and Bestor Robinson, as army officers, helped develop high-altitude and cold weather equipment.

After the war, the Sierra Club grew from a California based outings club into a national organization. Volunteers taught rock climbing and led trips until the early 1990s, when the expense

Jules Eichorn, Norman Clyde, Robert Underhill, Glen Dawson, August 16, 1931
PHOTO: Francis Farquhar from the Glen Dawson Collection

of insuring such trips all but eliminated the historic rock climbing section. Many of the displaced climbers went on to form the Southern California Mountaineers Association. New generations of climbers improved equipment and techniques to make bold first ascents in Yosemite, South America, Greenland and Asia. Modern guide books replaced the old. Climbing maps and literature can be viewed on the internet.

Today, every imaginable climbing record has been set for each 14,000-foot peak in California: by the shortest possible time; by the youngest or the oldest; one day ascents; solo climbs; from the lowest to the highest point; with dogs. Whatever the feat, the mountains are still there for all to enjoy and whatever you plan, this book will be helpful.

After the Palisades Climbing School in 1931: Jules Eichorn and Robert Underhill on the Milk Bottle, the summit block of Starlight Peak (14,200 feet) PHOTO: Glen Dawson

Introduction

Peter Croft

Mountaineering, what some call the sport of mountain climbing, could more accurately be described as the art of climbing mountains. The stark simplicity of the aim coupled with the multitude of divergent techniques and styles means that any ascent can be a personalized one. How one plans and executes one's ascent of this blank canvas of an idea determines how well you fit into the equation. By knowing all your options, understanding your own body and, just as importantly, using your imagination, climbing a mountain can be a true expression of who you are.

Eric Shipton and Bill Tilman, the great British exploratory mountaineers of the greater ranges in the 30's, 40's and 50's, believed that one should be able to plan an expedition on the back of an envelope. If you couldn't do that, they claimed, the whole enterprise had gotten just too complicated. In the wildest mapless regions of the Himalaya, Karakorum and Patagonia they put their idea of simple and lightweight trips to the test. Their streamlined strategy meant that they could be much more spur-of-the-moment in adapting to their condition dependent environment; much better able, for example, to take advantage of sudden and brief weather windows to either go for it OR run away to fight another day. Just as important they were far better able to be truly in touch with their chosen environment and themselves. Their example is especially fine food for thought in this day of lightweight gear and these mountains of (mostly) good weather.

The breathtakingly vast and complex High Sierra reaches its highest point in the massive form of Mt. Whitney. Known more widely as the highest in the lower 48, it has a lot more to recommend it than mere altitude. This mountain, more than any other I have visited in the entire range, is unique in its ability to show us such a multitude of very different faces and moods. Depending on the direction of approach, the weather or time of day, the peak can, by turns, appear benign, beautiful or ominously hostile. Viewed from the west Mt. Whitney is remarkably unremarkable, appearing as a long humpbacked peak. Circling around to the north the mountain grows increasingly impressive due in part to its steep, turreted flanks but even more for its classic profile that so clearly illustrates the trademark topography of the Sierra: a long and gradual incline sloping up from the west to the summit and then a sudden plunging escarpment to the east. A drive up the highways on either side of the range readily confirms it. On the west side rolling forested hills stretch lazily into the distance where half imagined peaks hover above the central valley haze. Motoring up the east side on Highway 395, however, there is nothing "rolling" or "half imagined" about it. It is from this perspective that Whitney achieves its full dramatic stature. In a rising swell of terraced cliffs, glacially gouged canyons and multi-spired summit ridge the spectacular nature of the range's highest peak brings a particular sense of reverent appreciation and breathless anticipation to the mountain traveller. Coming abreast of Whitney as you roll into Lone Pine, one is awed by the massive wall of mountains that marches away to the north, a wall so high and effectively complete as to block Pacific storms and create an entire desert in its shadow.

It is from here, the side that faces the rising sun, that Whitney reigns supreme. Just the drive up the Whitney Portal Road is a trip in itself: the expanding views, the changing vegetation and the cooling, clearing atmosphere in a panorama of peaks. As you

Peter Croft on the East Face of Mt. Whitney PHOTO: Galen Rowell/Mountain Light Gallery

crane your neck over the steering wheel it is impossible to take it all
in, all the more so for the white knuckle back seat passengers half
sobbing "For the love of God, watch the road!" In the thirteen miles
it takes to drive from Lone Pine on the valley floor to trailhead at
the Portal the change in elevation effects a change in temperature
and environment quite the equivalent of your changing you mind
and heading north instead all the way to Vancouver, Canada. That,
however, is only the beginning.

July 6, 1864

At last I reached the top, and, with the greatest caution, wormed my body over the brink, and rolling out upon the smooth surface of the granite, looked over and watched Cotter make his climb.

He came steadily up, with no sense of nervousness, until he got to the narrow part of the ice, and here he stopped and looked up with a forlorn face to me; and he asked if it had occurred to me that we had, by and by, to go down again.

We had now an easy slope to the summit, and hurried up over rocks and ice, reaching the crest at exactly twelve o'clock.

I rang my hammer upon the topmost rock; we grasped hands, and I reverently named the grand peak Mount Tyndall.

To our surprise, upon sweeping the horizon with my level, there appeared two peaks equal in height with us, and two rising even higher! That which looked highest of all was a cleanly cut helmet of granite upon the same ridge with Mount Tyndall, lying about six miles south, and fronting the desert with a bold square bluff which rises to the crest of the peak, where a white fold of snow trims it gracefully.

Mount Whitney, as we afterwards called it in honor of our chief, is probably the highest land within the United States.

Its summit looked glorious, but inaccessible.

Clarence King

Geologist, mountaineer, first director of the United States Geological Survey, noted for his explorations of the Sierra Nevada

Opposite: Mt. Whitney from the top of Mithral Dihedral on Mt. Russell
PHOTO: Dan Patitucci/Patitucci Photo

Robert "SP" Parker as John Muir on the one hundred and twenty-fifth anniversary reenactment of Muir's first ascent of the Mountaineer's Route. PHOTO: Andy Selters

Chapter One

The Story of Mt. Whitney

The Characters Who Came Before Us

Mt. Whitney was not always a lofty summit ogled by aspiring mountaineers. Five hundred million years ago it lay under an ocean, its summit rocks a marine locale much better suited to, say, jigging for cod or perhaps scuba diving and spear fishing, if only people had been invented at that time. The entire range really just began to rear up about thirty million years ago, something like the day before yesterday in geologic time. Just three million years ago major work began, uplifting the range to more or less what we see now. Even now, however, the work continues and the mountains grow, evidenced by the Owens Valley earthquake of 1872. On March 26 of that year a major quake ripped through the valley killing twenty nine people, leveling houses in Lone Pine and destroying the county courthouse in Independence. On the upside geologists reckon the entire range grew six feet taller that day.

Mountaineering in the Sierra Nevada began about one hundred and forty years ago, spurred on, surprisingly, by the California state legislature. Thanks to them an official survey was formed under the direction of Josiah Whitney ostensibly to look for gold and other precious metals. That, at least, was how it started. Before long, however, a few of the participants in the survey realized that this was a great opportunity to shirk their duties, go climbing and get paid for it. After all, who was to say whether or not there might be a pot of gold on the tops of those mountains. Mountaineering-wise, they had it made.

The Whitney Survey field party of 1864: Gardiner, Cotter, Brewer and King
PHOTO: The Bancroft Library, University of California, Berkeley

Clarence King was the most notable of these and perhaps the craftiest in his method of ensuring his continued funding. Upon spying the highest peak on the horizon he named it after the holder of purse strings, his boss Josiah Whitney. This stroke of genius ensured him the blessings of Josiah and the wherewithal to climb as he wished.

Clarence, though very strong and charismatic, had an unfortunate knack for climbing the wrong mountain. His first faux pas in his quest for the highest peak in the land occurred in 1864 when he and Dick Cotter climbed what they thought just had to be the tallest of them all. Part of a field party led by Professor William Brewer the two set off across terra incognita towards what they believed was the highest. Due to the unexplored and unmapped nature of the tortuous terrain just the approach to the peak was horrendous, full of maddening false starts, heart-dropping near misses and more or less constant epics. Commenting on these mountaineering voyages into the unknown, Professor Brewer may have exaggerated when he explained:

"It's easy enough to climb a mountain when you know where to go." Oh really? Well then, I suppose it's easy enough to be a rocket scientist if you simply know how.

But if the multi day trek towards their goal seemed perilous, climbing the peak sounded suicidal. Writing in his usual cliffhanger style, King described one desperate scene after another.

"Immense boulders were partly embedded in the ice just above us . . . trembling on the edge of a fall," and ". . . huge blocks thundered down past us . . . "

The climbing itself sounds horrendous, as well, as they ascended "smooth faces of granite, clinging simply by the cracks and protruding crystals of feldspar, and then hewed steps (with a great Bowie knife) up fearfully steep ice slopes, zig-zagging to the right and left to avoid the flying boulders." Later, a blank wall is overcome by shimmying up a column of ice, like a kid up a tree. This proved to be the key to the summit and, later, on the descent, as a source of despair when they found that it had fallen down. While on the summit, though, they discovered two peaks that were clearly higher, the highest a full six miles south. *Oops!* King's published account of the ascent is a hoot, particularly when compared to the rather sedate notes in the official report and the relative ease of later ascents. With food almost gone and their equipment in tatters they made their return journey. Cotter, whose shoes had blown out, shuffled along with his feet wrapped in blankets–more or less mountaineering in bedroom slippers.

Seven years later Clarence climbed a different "highest peak" when he and Paul Pinson climbed what he again thought was Mt. Whitney in the summer of 1871. Once again his pants-crappingly wild description relates how he "crept on hands and knees up over steep and treacherous ice-crests, where a slide would have swept me over a brink of the southern precipice," and later, the "unreliableness" of the cliff that "might, at any moment, give the deathfall to one who had not the coolness and muscular power at instant command." (I, myself, have reflected on the coolness and muscular power that was required when my dog PeeWee and I walked up the gently sloping peak just a few years ago.) On the cloudy summit he made a sheepish find–a small pile of rocks with an arrow stuck in it. Well, at least he was the first white man up

First to climb Mt. Whitney: Lone Pine residents Charles D. Begole, Albert H. Johnson and John Lucas (not pictured), Eastern California Museum Collection

there. But no, just a few years later it was discovered by a civil engineer named Goodyear that King had missed the big one again, this time by five miles. Well, at least he was getting closer. Apparently Goodyear considered Clarence something of a blabbermouthy show-off and took some pleasure in exposing his ineptitude. Hearing of his mountain-sized blunder King rushed back to correct his goof and finally summited the real Mt. Whitney in September 1873. It had to have been a bit of a bummer, however, when he discovered that he had been beaten to the top by two separate parties.

The first to the summit was a group of three fishermen from Lone Pine who got there just a month before Clarence–Charles Begole, Albert Johnson and John Lucas. The leader of a different party, a fellow named William Crapo, claimed that they were actually the first but this has generally been discounted. His flimsy evidence,

The Smithsonian summit shelter on Mt. Whitney, early 1900's.
Pictured (left to right) are Owens Valley residents William Parcher, William Chalfant, unknown,
Burton Frasher, Sr. and unknown. PHOTO: Eastern California Museum Collection

possibly along with the fact he later murdered a mailman, has led most historians to believe that Crapo was full of it.

A debate sprang up as to what to name this high and mighty mountain. Dome of Inyo was proposed by someone who, as far as I can tell, had never seen the peak from the Inyo County side. From there the spiky summit ridge looks nothing like a dome. The fishermen thought long and hard and came up with Fishermen's Peak, which is a dandy name coming from three sportsmen knocking back a few beers. There were some, though, who thought this name was too flippant and undignified, people with connections in high places and, perhaps, asses to kiss. These people came up with a couple of different names. Fowler's Peak was suggested by some fawning sycophant of Senator Fowler's. Imagine naming a beautiful mountain after a politician. Don't laugh, though, it almost happened. On April 1, 1881 a bill concerning the official name came before the Senate with the amendment proposing the mountain be called Fowler's Peak. The bill passed but the governor ended the April Fool's Day foolishness by vetoing the bill. Good for the governor!

It's hard to understand why so little imagination was used in the christening. Certainly the High Sierra is liberally sprinkled with wonderfully descriptive names: Temple Crag, the Palisades, the Minarets, Bear Creek Spire, Cathedral Peak and the Incredible Hulk are just some of my favorites. The local Paiute Indians had an almost hippyish flair for place names. Their sense of spiritual connectedness to the land is obvious with the names they gave for many prominent Sierra peaks. Forty miles to the north is Mount Sill (a sacred mountain for them) which they called Guardian of the Valley. It sounds even better in their language: Nee-na-mee-shee. Now that's a great name. Their name for Mt. Whitney was Too-man-go-yah which means very old man. This "old man" was a spirit that lived inside the mountain who was responsible for the future of the tribe. Hanging out on the summit ten thousand feet above the valley floor he was ideally situated to look out and observe what the locals were up to.

But in the end it was the employees of Josiah Whitney who won out and the highest mountain in the lower 48 states was named after a man who had never been there.

Clarence King might have missed out on the mountain's first ascent but he was the one to discover it and bring the mountain into the public light. His popular and amazing stories may have included more than a few epic exaggerations but they were nonetheless inspiring tales and he was hardly the last mountaineer to spice up the truth.

In October of the same year, just a couple months after the mountain's first ascent, the naturalist John Muir climbed what has come to be known as the Mountaineer's Route up the fearsome looking eastern escarpment. His accounts of his High Sierra climbing was much different than Kings, usually underplaying the difficulties and instead focusing on the beauty of the natural world he was travelling through. His focus and insight into the mountains led him to the rather landmark discovery that Yosemite Valley was formed by glacial action, an idea that was diametrically opposed to the generally accepted one put forth by no other than Josiah Whitney (he believed the Valley was created by an earthquake.) Upon hearing of Muir's so called discovery, a pissed off Josiah labeled Muir an ignoramus. In hindsight (the glacier theory, after all, proved to be correct) Muir might well have countered "I know you are, but what am I?" but he declined to bandy words. Josiah seems to have made a habit of making bold statements, fancying himself a bit of a geological smartypants. He brazenly declared that the summit of Yosemite's Half Dome ". . . never has been, and never will be, trodden by human foot." Try telling that to the zillion people who have eaten peanut butter and jelly sandwiches on top. Muir may not have had Whitney's educational pedigree but he based his observations on a life spent in the wilds. The mountains were his university and, as he liked to say, his church. And it is thanks to his conservationist efforts that Yosemite National Park was created.

In July of 1904, in what must have been a rock busting beast of an effort, Gustave Marsh completed the Mt. Whitney Trail. He was no park service employee or government lackey, however, and really it was Gustave alone who envisioned, fundraised and led the construction itself. A man of real creative vision he foresaw the importance of Mt. Whitney as a tourist attraction and as a site for high altitude science. Four years after the trail was completed the Smithsonian Institute employed Marsh to build a summit shelter for various high altitude experiments. In 1909 the stone building was completed and for many years it was the highest such research station in the world. One can imagine the Lone Pine townspeople of the early 1900s peering out their windows on stormy nights, nervously looking on as lightning nailed the summit laboratory, wondering what sort of Frankensteinian experiments were really going on up there.

The next big evolutionary step in the mountain's mountaineering maturity occurred when the peak's East Face was climbed. In 1931 Robert Underhill, Glen Dawson, Jules Eichorn and Norman Clyde ascended the biggest wall on the tallest peak in the lower 48 states. Clyde became a legend among Sierra mountaineers having made something like 120 first ascents in the range–more than anyone else, by a long shot. Almost as impressive, and certainly more jaw dropping, was the size and contents of the pack he carried. Thinking nothing of carrying 100 lbs, he would tote such obvious (?) necessities as a couple of fishing rods, a cast iron frying pan, several pairs of boots, an anvil to repair those boots and an axe. On top of that, however, he would also saddle himself with a small library of hardback books in foreign languages, several pistols, a rifle and as many as five cameras. He was known as an eccentric which is a pretty sedate way to put it. Today's lightweight alpinist would treat any climber with half those peculiarities like a rat chewing lunatic and give him a wide berth. Certainly the FBI would hunt down any and all persons hiding out in the backcountry with a similar arsenal of weapons.

Clyde's climbing pals were a mixed group. Robert Underhill was from out east, a philosophy prof and Appalachian Mountain Club member who was a major player in the introduction of technical mountaineering to this country. His influence came both through his climbs and through his important articles on the subject. Glen Dawson and Jules Eichorn, on the other hand, were two teenage tigers from California who already rated amongst the very best climbers in the country. Any Sierra mountaineer of today is familiar with their names. Landmark climbs of theirs included Eichorn's' ascent of the spectacularly exposed Higher Cathedral Spire which ushered in modern technical climbing to Yosemite, Dawson's ascent of the Mechanic's Route at Tahquitz Rock which was the country's toughest rock climb at the time and the relatively unknown (but

Trailside meadow along the Whitney Trail   PHOTO: Corinne Newton

distinctly hair raising) traverse between Middle Palisade and Norman Clyde Peak. These youngsters were so chomping at the bit, they had to be talked down from having a crack at a much harder direct finish on the Whitney climb.

Upon arrival at Iceberg Lake the four climbers were at first awed by the prospect, but once on the face they found the climbing much easier than expected and, climbing in two parties of two, raced up the route in a little over three hours.

This climb, although not extraordinarily difficult, pointed the way to future developments in the range. Up until then Sierra mountaineers had mostly scrambled up peaks by their easiest routes. Now, a whole new world was opening up.

In 1960 Yosemite style big wall climbing came to the Whitney area when El Capitan pioneer Warren Harding climbed Keeler Needle's 1,500 foot east face. Hardly overawed, Harding and pal Glen Denny invited two rank beginners along for the climb because "they were good wine drinkers." It probably made pretty good sense to Warren, who was notoriously fond of red wine, and the four man "party" reached the top after three days on the wall.

The first winter ascent of Keeler's east face took place twelve years later when Harding himself, Tim Auger and hyperactive Galen Rowell climbed the wall in March of 1972. Rowell went on to become the most important Whitney pioneer in more recent times. In fact, Galen's name has become synonymous with Sierra climbing due to his insatiable appetite for new climbs throughout the range. From the 1970s right up until the time of his untimely death in a plane crash in 2001 this great mountaineer and adventure photojournalist made innumerable visits to the area. From hand numbing/teeth chattering winter ascents and harrowing ski descents (he was not the most elegant skier) to new routes and first free ascents, Galen treated the area like his own backyard. And from the first free ascent of Keeler Needle to the first ski descent of the Mountaineer's Route to new routes throughout the entire Whitney region he was, quite simply, an animal. At 60, his unbridled energy and enthusiasm still led him adventuring around the world like a kid in a global candy store. I was lucky enough to call him my friend and sometimes went climbing with him.

In 1999 he and I made a one day winter ascent of the East Face of Whitney. Conditions were very dry and we able to climb the mountain much as we would on a summer ramble (although it was pretty damn chilly in the shade). What struck me was how lighthearted the whole "winter" ascent was. Clad in jogging pants, a sweatshirt and running shoes we hiked in like two schoolboys skipping school and climbed as if we were getting away with something that was naughty. Nonstop fun. Climbing with Galen was unique. Good-natured and ruthlessly fit, he was savant-like in his wide ranging and deep understanding of the workings of the world and he would often hold forth in the middle of cruxy situations, explaining his complex theories while reaching for the next hold. Although I climbed first, my intellect could never keep up with his and I would laughingly claim to understand in the vain hope of shutting him up. An integral and important part of Galen was his brilliant photography. He used his images to enlighten people not only of the worlds' natural beauty but also of critical issues that threaten it. With his camera strapped to his chest in a quick release harness he was as fast on the draw as they come. Years after our Whitney climb I saw a collection of photos from that day, completely unaware that he had been taking them. Today those pictures are a clear-eyed connection not only to Galen but also to the notion that climbing mountains makes us more alive.

When reading mountaineering histories it's easy to come to the conclusion that the importance of climbing lies solely in the desperate struggles by bigger-than-life heroes. The reality is quite different. Moments like on that winter ascent with Galen are as sharp and clear a memory as some of my most difficult climbs. Great days in the mountains with good friends are times that are embedded in our psyche, things that can't help but have an effect on who we are. Frosty mornings, orange alpenglow and clear skies so blue you seem to be half way to outer space are just a few of the ingredients that make the mountains such a special environment. Surrounded by sparkling granite and an endless horizon, climbing a mountain with a close friend is about as good a way as any to discover answers to questions you'd never think to ask in the humdrum of every day life. The real importance of mountain climbing lies in what the mountains ask of each of us and what they give to us in return. The most important histories are the ones we get to keep.

"The supreme joy I felt when I realized that my prayer had been answered, and that I was at last really standing on the summit of Mount Whitney, knew no bounds.
For the time being I forgot that I was ever tired; one glance was enough to compensate for all the trials of the trip.
How strange it seemed to be looking off for a distance of seventy miles down into Death Valley, the lowest point...
Oh what an inspiration it was to look from that magnificent peak on the grand panorama of mountains, reaching from beyond the Yosemite to San Bernardino!
Range after range in every direction, peak on peak, comprising almost limitless forms, rise one above the other, each striving for the mastery."

Anna Mills
One of the four first women to climb Mt. Whitney, 1878

Women climbers at the summit cairn on Mt. Whitney, circa 1880
Eastern California Museum Collection

Chapter Two

Mt. Whitney Natural History Primer

Geology

550 to 410 million years ago, during the early Paleozoic Era, the Sierra Nevada, as we know it now, was covered by seawater. Marine sedimentary rocks were deposited during that time. Remnants of these ancient rocks are still present in the Sierra Nevada to the north of Mt. Whitney.

Approximately 400 million years ago, collisions between the North American Plate, and its neighboring plate resulted in folding and faulting of the marine rocks deposited earlier. This event is called the Antler orogeny (a geologic term for an episode of mountain building). The Antler orogeny resulted in the development of a mountain chain east of the present Sierra Nevada. During the following 25 million years of subsidence and erosion, the Antler Mountains eroded away and a new ocean basin formed.

Durig the Late Permian and Early Triassic periods, approximately 250 to 350 million years ago, a collision occurred between the North American Plate and one or more of its neighbors. This event, which took place at a time when dinosaurs were becoming a dominant life form on the planet, is called the Sonoma orogeny. The Sonoma orogeny further deformed the existing rocks in the area and caused regional uplift in central Nevada. Basins formed on either side of this uplift, including the area of the present day Sierra Nevada. The stage was now set for a great mountain building event.

About 220 to 215 million years ago, the North American Plate changed direction forcing the adjacent oceanic plate to the west to get shoved or "subducted" beneath the North American Plate. This caused volcanism in the region.

Following a five million year period of relative inactivity, further collision occurred during the Jurassic Period, about 210 million years ago. Tear-dropped shaped bodies of molten rock called "plutons" ascended through the crust due to their light density. These plutons shoved aside the existing rock, and as they reached the surface, crystallized due to decreasing heat and pressure. The greatest period of emplacement of these plutons was during the late Jurassic and Cretaceous Periods, 210 to 80 million years ago. These are the granitic rocks we see throughout the Sierra Nevada today. Mountain building occurred along with the plutonic emplacement, known as the Nevadan orogeny. An ancestral mountain range in the area of the present-day Sierra Nevada had been built.

As the Nevadan orogeny winded down and ended, erosion began to occur in the Sierra Nevada region. The Nevadan mountains eventually eroded to a chain of gently rolling hills, probably much similar in appearance to the present-day foothills of the Sierra Nevada to the west.

Then about 30 million years ago, renewed uplift began to occur in the Sierra Nevada region. By 20 million years ago, the Sierra Nevada had tilted to the west. Volcanism occurred in the Sierra Nevada to the north. About three million years ago, major uplift of the Sierra Nevada began, resulting in the massive escarpment along the Sierra Nevada that we see today. At the present time, uplift continues and was dramatically displayed during the 1872 Owens Valley earthquake. It is thought that the Sierra Nevada uplifted at least six feet in elevation.

As the surface was lifted, drainage to the west and the east led to stream erosion, forming the great canyons of the Sierra. In the

Whitney summit shelter PHOTO: Pete Yamagata

Whitney region, a long north-south faultline, west of the summit ridge disrupted the stream formation and the westerly streams from the crest found it easier to follow the fault to the south, forming Kern River Canyon. Following the last uplift and continuing until the past 10,000 years was the planing of the ice-age glaciers, changing the V-shaped river canyons to the present U-shaped glacial canyons. This is quite noticeable in upper Lone Pine Canyon. The piles of rubble (moraines) may be seen near Whitney Portal. Glaciers do not carve out a single smooth slope, but due to the quarrying effect caused by the fracture of granite blocks, scoop out steps or benches. Whitney Portal, Lone Pine Lake, Whitney Outpost, and Mirror Lake are examples of such glacial scoops. Mt. Whitney's summit is a remnant land surface left over from the gently rolling hills that were first uplifted about 30 million years ago.

Looking across Mt. Whitney from the west to the Inyo Mountains. PHOTO: China Lake NAWS

The igneous rocks may be divided into two large groups, the acidic or light colored rocks (light both in color and weight) and the basic or dark-colored rocks. Basalt, of which the great lava flows near Little Lake are composed, is the most common basic rock.

The light rocks vary greatly in appearance. If the molten magma is suddenly cooled, crystals are not formed and the rock becomes volcanic glass or obsidian. If the cooling is a little slower, microscopic crystals are formed, creating rhyolite. In normal cooling beneath the surface, the crystals are 0.1 to 0.2 inches long and the rock is granite. If the cooling is still slower, much larger crystals appear in the rock, and it then carries the additional title of porphyry. Yet all of these rocks have the same chemical composition. In general, granite consists of quartz, feldspar, micas, and small amounts of other minerals such as garnet. If quartz is missing, the rock is called monzonite. If a little quartz is present, it becomes quartz monzonite. It is of these monzonites that Mt. Whitney is formed. It is the feldspar in these rocks that gives Mt. Whitney its very notable pinkish-white appearance which is so striking in the light of the setting sun.

Flora & Fauna

The types of plants and animals found in the Whitney region can be classified by changes in climate and elevation, known as life zones. As a comparison, travelling north from the equator or up from sea level, the climate becomes colder. Roughly speaking, a rise in elevation of 1,000 feet is equivalent to a northward journey, across latitudes, of 300 miles. From Owens Lake in the southern Owens Valley to the summit of Mt. Whitney is a gain of almost 11,000 feet, representing a climatic change equivalent to what one would find traveling the distance between Mazatlan, Mexico and Nome, Alaska.

In the late nineteenth century, C. Hart Merriam developed the life zone system for classifying vegetation based on climactic data found in changes of elevation and latitude. The life zone system, which has been used for decades since its initial development, was a way to describe any given geographic area based on vegetation type and the amount of precipitation (rainfall) the area in question received. Each life zone was named after a geographical area which had temperatures similar to those areas observed by Merriam as he traveled from the bottom of Grand Canyon (Lower Sonoran life zone) to the tops of the San Francisco Peaks (Arctic-Alpine life zone) outside of Flagstaff, Arizona. Merriam's life zone system made the connection between elevation and latitude, but because it was based on climate–temperature and precipitation–its relevance was applicable to only the American southwest.

In the decades following Merriam's concept of life zones, several other systems for identifying plant communities were proposed and put into use. One of these was the concept of biomes, proposed by ecologists Frederic Clements and Victor Shelford shortly before World War II. A biome was described as an ecosystem where differences in temperature and precipitation created a unique community of plants and animals. In 1959, Philip Munz and David Keck developed the classification system of plant communities, a very broad system of classification based on the dominant plant species that occupy any given area. This system has achieved a great deal of popularity and is the one currently preferred by California ecologists.

Lone Pine Creek flows from snow banks high on the Sierra crest in the Arctic-Alpine life zone or Alpine community, until the waters sink into the desert sands in the Lower Sonoran life zone or Sagebrush Scrub community. All of this takes place in some fifteen miles along the Whitney Portal Road. The distance traveled from Lone Pine to road's end and the beginning of the Whitney Trail, is comparable to traveling from the southwest to the Canadian border, from high desert juniper and pinyon to Jeffrey pine and red fir.

The Whitney Trail soon crosses into the Canadian life zone, the lodgepole pine-red fir forest community. Beyond this, mountain hemlock, with its unique horizontal branches, replaces the white fir. At Mirror Lake, is the Hudsonian life zone or Subalpine forest community, with the lodgepole pine only growing in sheltered places. Continuing up and along the trail is the white pine region. By the time the Consultation Lake junction is reached, only the white-bark pine remains, and the *Albicaulis*, hugging the ground and growing but a few inches a year. Above Consultation, a few shrubs struggle, and finally, the only "tree" left is the alpine willow which grows to the magnificent height of just four inches.

The native animals range higher during the summer, in amongst the rocks along the trail. Mountain lions, black bears, mule deer and coyote are the largest mammals in the Sierra. There are also fox and a wide array of birds, amphibians, and snakes. The Clark's nutcracker, related to the raven, can be bold, flying down to camp looking for handouts. During the summer along the trail though,

Mt. Whitney Plant Communities

Elevation	Community	Life Zone
14,000'	Alpine	Arctic-Alpine
10,000'	Subalpine Forest	Hudsonian
	Lodgepole-Red Fir Forest	Canadian
	Yellow Pine Forest	Transition
		Upper Sonoran
	Desert Chaparral	
	Lower Chaparral	
		Lower Sonoran
3,000'	Alkali Sink Creosote Bush Sagebrush Scrub	

the most commonly seen mammal is the marmot, a large beaver-like woodchuck with a sharp whistle that might startle you as he (or they!) announces your arrival in his domain. Sometimes, a marmot might return a human whistle and carry on a conversation, but it's always a warning to other marmots that their territory has been penetrated and to be wary. Pikas, which resemble tiny, short-eared rabbits, no more than seven inches in length are often seen darting in and out of the holes between rocks.

On the summit of Whitney, in the Arctic-Alpine life zone or Alpine community, down among the cracks between the rocks, are nestled tiny wildflower gardens, their blooms just inches above the ground. Summer insects buzz around collecting pollen.

Along some parts of the trail the life zones are not so neatly cut. Lone Pine Canyon is an great place to observe "floral micro-

climates," small patches of plants that differ from the surrounding plant growth. Flowers may bloom in shaded places, while the surrounding meadow grasses have already turned brown. In the lower canyon, a long tongue of aspen and pines extends far down along the creek bed into the pinyon-juniper community. At Whitney Portal, the pines and firs form a complete stand, while half a mile further up the trail, we pass into a chaparral-covered slope, exposed, void of any trees, where the sun shines bright and hot on a cloudless day. At the same level, a few yards to the left, under the shading cliffs of Mt. Candlelight (12,000'+), the conifers extend along the stream bed. Imagine how many hikers have

Lone Pine Lake. PHOTO: Kathleen Hession

looked longingly at the deep shade of the pines, as while struggling along in the heat and dust just a few feet away.

There are many opportunities to study the entire series of life zones of the northern hemisphere in the short distance from Highway 395 to the Whitney Crest.

Lone Pine Creek and its many lakes provide excellent fishing, in spite of the heavy usage they receive. The North Fork of Lone Pine Creek (approach to the technical routes in this book for Whitney and Russell) and the higher lakes, Consultation and Iceberg, are more remote and are more likely to produce a good catch.

First discovered in the headwaters of the South Fork of the Kern River, the golden trout, the state fish of California, was introduced into the Cottonwood Lakes in 1893. Since that time, it has been planted in many of the high lakes of the Sierra. A close relative, the rainbow trout, also a California native, has likewise been widely planted in this area, and the two have interbred so that all shades from golden to white may now be taken. The Mt. Whitney Hatchery, near Independence, has cultured these, as well as the Eastern brook and the brown trout.

Along the switchbacks on the Whitney Trail   PHOTO: Galen Rowell/Mountain Light Gallery

Chapter Three

Gearing up for the Mt. Whitney Trail

What you really need to know before you go

Whitney *Portal*–like the word suggests–really is a gateway: a cool, pine scented threshold where there's a feeling in the air that the adventure has already begun. Huge cliffs rise right out of the canyon's floor but instead of closing in and darkening the Portal the blazing white granite actually illuminates it. Tall evergreens line the rushing creek, providing a soothing shadow on even the hottest of days. My favorite times there are the early mornings– still dark with a lighter strip of peach colored glow to the east. By headlamp making last minute adjustments to my pack while nearby others do the same–all of us whispering and checking our gear like pirates planning a dawn raid.

My second most favorite times and by far the most delicious are the late afternoon returns to the Whitney Portal Store for hamburgers and french fries.

Weather

The High Sierra can boast of having possibly the friendliest weather conditions of any mountain range on the planet. In the summer season long periods of settled weather are the norm. I remember one summer guiding in Tuolomne when we hit the hundred day mark with no rain. Of course bad weather can occur any time of the year but so can good weather. I've climbed an almost summer-like Whitney (14,496 ft) in January wearing running shoes and, conversely, woken up to six inches of snow in Yosemite Valley (4,000 ft.) in June.

The most likely bad weather scenarios you're likely to encounter during the summer months are thunderstorms. These can happen at any time but are, by far, most frequent in the afternoon. Very early starts (getting up pre-dawn) are a particularly good idea if there is the slightest chance of thunderstorm activity. If during the morning clouds begin building you should strongly consider abandoning your climb for the day. The local ranger stations are the best single source of information for mountain and trail conditions. As well you can check local newspapers and radio stations for the forecast but keep in mind that forecasting in the Sierra is more difficult than in the lowlands–mountains create their own weather. It's up to you to be aware of that weather and be ready to hightail it if necessary. Caught in the teeth of an unexpected storm you'll find there is no consolation in whining, "But the weatherman said . . ."

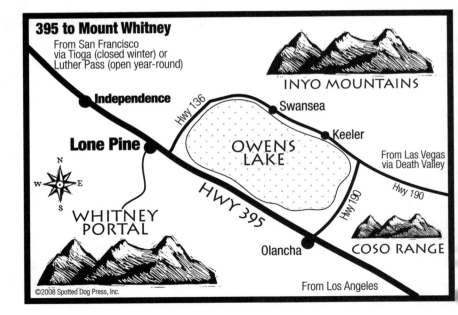

395 to Mount Whitney

From San Francisco via Tioga (closed winter) or Luther Pass (open year-round)

INYO MOUNTAINS

Independence

Hwy 136

Swansea

Keeler

Lone Pine

OWENS LAKE

From Las Vegas via Death Valley

N

W   E

S

HWY 395

Hwy 190

Hwy 190

WHITNEY PORTAL

Olancha

COSO RANGE

©2008 Spotted Dog Press, Inc.

From Los Angeles

Getting There

If you are flying to California, the most direct major airports to Mt. Whitney/Lone Pine are, in order: Bob Hope Airport-Burbank/Glendale; Ontario International; then Los Angeles International; followed by McCarran International in Las Vegas; Reno/Tahoe International in Reno, Nevada; Sacramento, Oakland, then San Francisco, California. Currently, there is no commercial passenger air service to Lone Pine, so plan on driving at least 200 miles one-way from the closest airport. If you rent a car, buy the extra insurance (bears). Best year-round road access is from the south, Bob Hope, Ontario and LAX. An occasional flash flood in the Mojave Desert is a minor concern. In winter, most passes across the Sierra are closed. Chains are often required on 395 southbound from Reno. There are three main passes on 395 between Reno and Bishop: Devil's Gate, Conway Summit (8,138 ft., 2,480 m., the highest point on 395 between San Diego and Canada) and Deadman Summit, all subject to winter road closure.

Parking

Parking is available at the Whitney Portal trailhead for both day and overnight use. Backpackers and moonlight hikers must park in the overnight area. Overflow parking is on the south shoulder of the road, 500 feet east of the overnight area. Park in a designated area, clear of the roadway, securely setting your parking brake and blocking a wheel. Lock your vehicle and don't leave food or any scented items in, under or near your car! Bears are active in the area and looking for food. We have seen many cars with major body damage! Rangers look inside vehicles and will write tickets for improper food storage. Store anything you are not taking into the backcountry in one of the brown food storage lockers located at trailheads, parking areas and campgrounds including: food, sealed drinks, coolers, water bottles, toiletries (toothpaste, soap, shampoo, deodorant) and scented items.

Proper Storage of Food at the Trailhead

Before setting out on the trail make absolutely sure you have left absolutely no food in your car. Bears have no problem detecting anything snackable and seem to actually enjoy breaking into your car (we've seen them do it.) Rangers as well have little difficulty spying out food items in your vehicle and while they won't bust your car window for a quick snack they can, and sometimes will, issue you a ticket with a fine. I once returned to my car after a day in the mountains to find a ticket taped to my windshield. In official sounding language it leveled the serious charge of improper food storage–specifically half of a single peanut in my back seat. I was lucky and got off with a warning. If you do have any food that you aren't taking on the trail make sure to leave it in one of the food storage boxes at the trailhead.

At high camps the main threat comes from marmots, wiener dog-sized rodents that are much like guinea pigs on steroids. These cute little bastards will chew through packs and tents to get at food items or anything with salt on it. This means that you not only have to store your food properly but also anything that has sweat on it. Bear canisters are the obvious way to protect the food but for sweat crusted packs or hats etc. you'll need to be a bit creative. Either hang them up in a tree or take a stick and climb on top of a boulder or small cliff. Weight one end with rocks leaving the other end poking out over the edge and hang your stuff on that.

Bear Canisters

Bear-resistant food canisters, small black containers that fit in or strap to a backpack, are now required for overnight trips on many Sierra trails including the Mt. Whitney Trail. The canisters, which hold about six days worth of food, well-planned and tightly packed for two, can be purchased or rented from the USFS and various outdoor retailers. The old counter-balance method of food storage in the backcountry–hoisting bags of food up onto tree branches–does not work at all anymore. Bears have had years of experience in figuring out how to get the food down.

Adult Black Bears *(Ursus americanus)* weigh up to 350 pounds and will do major damage. They know that it is a lot easier to feed themselves from improperly stored food, garbage or any kind of scented items left in a car, cooler, tent, or backpack than to forage in nature. Once a bear has obtained these items, it becomes dependent on human food sources, and begins to lose its natural fear of people. Improper food storage has become a major problem and because of this, encounters with bears in popular backcountry campsites are common. Tenacious bears, attracted by the smell of food, will hang around campsites for hours.

One guy came back from a climb of Whitney to find that a bear had walked on the roof of his sports utility vehicle, crumpling it, and had ripped off a passenger door just to get a package of cookies that was *under* the car wrapped in a garbage bag topped with rocks. Had this fellow used the bear boxes at the trailhead this incident would have been avoided.

A sow (female bear) was killed because she had lost her inherent fear of humans. We are the only ones who can keep bears and other Sierra species wild and alive, beginning with proper food storage. Minimize the amount of food you bring to Whitney Portal before you arrive. Whenever you leave your vehicle, even if just for a few minutes, store all food and scented items in the food storage lockers at the trailhead.

The Essentials

Mt. Whitney has been climbed by hikers in all types of clothing and as many types of shoes. Bikinis and sandals have been worn, but chances of success are greater with synthetic clothing designed for the outdoors–nylon, pile and polypropylene. Though Sierra summer days may start out sunny and beautiful without a cloud in the sky, by early afternoon, thunderheads may be building up across the crest. If trapped by a sudden Sierra storm, it is not your comfort, but possibly your life that may be at stake. Every daypack or backpack should contain a basic list of items:

- Plain water or sports drink and snacks
- Headlamp, spare bulbs and batteries
- Lightweight, layered clothing to include rain jacket/pants that can also double as a windbreaker; lightweight synthetic underwear–tops and bottoms; synthetic or wool sweater
- Pocket knife
- Map (and compass, if you know how to use it)
- Matches in waterproof container or plastic baggie
- Sunglasses, sunscreen
- Hat
- First aid kit

Additional equipment is discussed in greater detail in the following paragraphs.

Water & Electrolytes

With the exception of the North Fork, there is no water on the first two miles of the main Whitney Trail. There is water on the way to Trail Camp, but because of *Giardia*, water should be filtered. Water filters, available from outdoor stores, are typically used on overnight backpacking trips when it's not convenient to carry the additional weight of bottled water. In a pinch, water purifying tablets can be used or water boiled, but filtering is the most effective way to weed out out *Giardia* cysts. Dayhikers may want to carry their own water, a minimum of three to four quarts during the summer. Include a bottle of Gatorade or other sports drink, or packets of electrolyte replacement powder like Gookinaid or Cytomox which will replenish the body's electrolytes, salts and minerals lost through perspiration. For some people, a quart of sports drink can mean the difference between a severe headache and weakness from dehydration to feeling great.

Campfires & Cooking Stoves

Norman Clyde, the great California mountaineer, who made more than fifty ascents of Mt. Whitney from every possible route and angle, was famous for carrying a pack that weighed over a hundred pounds. Among the items he carried were a large cast iron skillet for frying up fresh trout, a fishing rod, a cobbler's kit for repairing the nails on his "hobnailed" hiking boots, a firearm of some sort for hunting, a full size axe—you get the picture. Lightweight stoves have since replaced the iron skillet; the one-person bivy sack has replaced the two-person tent, and tube-fed neoprene water pouches worn on the back have replaced conventional water bottles.

Campfires are prohibited in the entire Mt. Whitney Zone, so a small backpacking stove is essential, unless you are planning to carry food that doesn't need cooking. Think lightweight. One pot and a mug for overnight trips. Use the pot for boiling water. Freeze-dried foods can be cooked in their own packaging. Add water to instant drinks and oatmeal in your mug. There's nothing more unpleasant than having a cup of morning coffee with water that has been boiled in a pot steeped in the residues of last night's burned seafood jumbalaya. Broth, decaffeinated tea or coffee, or pre-packaged powdered soups are a good way to rehydrate the body's lost liquids and salts.

Carry a mix of salty, sweet, and bland foods because elevation changes the body's physical condition and what you can or cannot eat. What is appealing at sea level may not be the same at 12,000

Corinne Newton travels lights as she starts up the Ebersbacher Ledges on the North Fork Approach
PHOTO: Scott Newton

feet. On a nauseous stomach, saltine crackers and broth may be more appealing than vegetarian lasagna. Include foods that don't require cooking, like power bars, muffins, bagels, dried fruit, salted pistachios or cashews, trail mix, and smoked jerky.

Food

Food is strictly a matter of personal preference. Lightweight freeze-dried foods are easy to cook in their own packaging. Some people like to plan meals and enjoy backcountry gourmet cooking. Whatever your taste, food requires twice as long to cook at altitude. At 5,000 feet, a ten minute cooking time at sea-level is twenty minutes; at 10,000 feet, cooking time is forty minutes, and at 12,000 feet, cooking time is over an hour.

Carry about eight ounces of protein per person per day: smoked jerky, canned chicken, tuna, low-fat or fat-free cheese, nuts, and about eight ounces of carbohydrates: crackers, rolls, cookies, candy. Include fruit like apples, dried peaches, pineapple, or small cans of fruit cocktail in light syrup. Many people have trouble digesting fats and oils at high altitude. Avoid fried foods, especially on the morning of the summit dash.

Clothing

From about mid-June to mid-September, the climate of Mt. Whitney is usually mild, clear and sunny. There are years when general travel on the main Whitney Trail doesn't begin until well into July because of a heavy snow year like that of 2004-2005.

Clothing is more often needed for protection from the sun than from the cold. A sea-level suntan is little protection against the ultraviolet light present at 14,000 feet. Dress for any backcountry trip in layers since the weather can change dramatically. Layers of clothing can be added or removed as conditions change. A warm Sierra morning, where a tee-shirt and shorts are perfect gear, can by afternoon turn into a cold, downpour requiring a sweater, rain jacket and rain pants.

A light, long-sleeved shirt, long pants or shorts, a brimmed hat and a good pair of UV blocking sunglasses make up the usual clothing. Sunscreen should be carried for face and lips. If you wear a tee-shirt and shorts, it's a good idea to carry a pair of lightweight synthetic underwear, a long-sleeve top and bottoms, as well as a lightweight rain jacket and a pair of rain pants. When traveling in the Sierra backcountry, raingear is an essential item to have in your daypack or backpack. Carry a synthetic or wool sweater or light-weight down parka. Wool and synthetic fibers dry more quickly than cotton and are better insulators if wet. Cotton materials, on the other hand, hold in moisture when wet and are almost impossible to dry out without the aid of the sun. Most Sierra thunderstorms show up with little or no warning, and during the summer, after-noon storms can be a daily occurrence. Dressing in layers with a parka or synthetic sweater covered by a rain jacket and a pair of rain pants will mean the difference between comfort and misery.

Footgear
Proper care of your feet is really important and can make or break a trip. This means wearing both adequate shoes and socks. Lightweight walking boots or trail running shoes are popular on dayhikes. Hiking boots are good on loose scree, talus, in deep snow and for people who need the additional ankle support on the trail. Wear high quality hiking socks (wool/synthetic blend). On over-night trips, carry extra dry, clean socks to prevent blisters. Using clean socks and lavishly taping potential hot spots with moleskin or tape before getting on the trail will help prevent blisters.

GorTex Sleeping Bag, Tent or Bivy Sack
Carry a sleeping bag on overnight trips. Lightweight is the way to go. Down is the lightest, warmest and most expensive. Synthetic bags are heavier than down, but will keep you warm. Forget car-camping-style sleeping bags. (Do they even make these

anymore?) With canvas exteriors and flannel-over-Dacron interiors they are way too bulky and heavy for any backpacking trip and take forever to dry out if soaked. Use a Thermarest or ensolite pad for padding, with an optional lightweight plastic or nylon ground cloth beneath the pad for insulation.

A bivy sack that slips over a sleeping bag provides fairly waterproof, wind-resistant coverage and is a lightweight alternative to carrying a tent on overnight trips. GorTex bivy sacks weigh less than two pounds and can withstand short-term inclement weather. They slip right over a sleeping bag and are roomy enough to allow the user to cook a meal and perform other "armchair" chores, while enjoying the toasty warmth of the sleeping bag inside. A bivy sack by itself can provide excellent shelter on unexpected overnight stays and have done so on some of the highest peaks in the world. Where speed and weight are key, and no major storms are on the horizon, a GorTex bag, bivy sack and bag or just a bivy sack are the way to go.

Single wall tents for two weigh under five pounds. The tent parts can be split up between the hiking partners to share the weight.

Pack
For overnight trips, an internal or external frame backpack is needed. For years, external frame packs were the only style of pack on the market. Internal frame packs provide a compact, weight-balanced and low-centered load, allowing for increased speed and greater comfort on the trail.

Flashlight, First Aid & A Camera
Carry a headlamp with an extra bulb and batteries for the unexpected after-dark return. Take a camera with extra film to record the summit victory. The views from the Whitney Crest and the "windows" above Trail Crest are absolutely fabulous!

Include a small first aid kit, with moleskin and adhesive tape. Apply moleskin or tape before you hit the trail to help prevent blistering from the onset. Carry aspirin or acetaminophen (the latter is gentler on stomachs) for possible high-altitude headaches and an antacid for nausea. Drinking a lot of water with electrolyte additive or a quart or two of sports drink will help minimize headaches and nausea, the symptoms of dehydration and altitude.

From late July to the end of September, technical climbing gear is generally not needed on the Whitney Trail. However, from late fall to early summer, depending on conditions (check with the Mt. Whitney Ranger District prior to your climb for current conditions), an ice axe and crampons are needed as well as the knowledge on how to use them—this is mountaineering, which requires training and skill. The snowpack during the winter of 2004-2005 was over 200% of historical averages in many places, with snow on the Mt. Whitney Trail well into July and on the high passes, into August.

Wilderness Sanitation–Pack it Out!

In the not too distant past, there was nothing more frustrating then spending all day getting to a scenic spot only to discover rock piles with streamers of toilet paper blowing in the wind or improperly buried toilet paper that had been dug up by some poor animal in search of a meal. A forest once burned to the ground by a fire started by a backcountry user trying to burn their toilet paper *(August 1997, Angeles National Forest, Narrows Fire)*. Human feces contain bacteria as well as the famed backcountry parasite, *Giardia lamblia*. Together, they are a large contributor to the contamination of backcountry water sources.

We are happy to report that the Inyo National Forest now requires all Mt. Whitney Zone visitors to do what canyoneers and backcountry boaters have been doing for years: pack out their solid human waste. As of this printing, complimentary, lightweight *Wag bag waste kits (wag: waste alleviation and gelling)* are available at

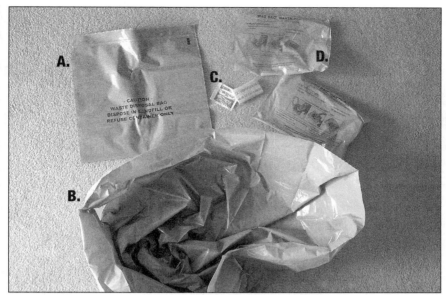

A. Zip-close disposal bag; B. Waste bag with gelling agent, odor neutralizer & decay catalyst
C. One antiseptic fresh nap and one package of toilet paper; D. Actual Wag Bag waste kits

the InterAgency Visitor Center in Lone Pine, the White Mountain Ranger Station in Bishop and the Crabtree Ranger Station. The kit (above) is easy to use. One kit can be carefully used 2-3 times:

Open the Wag Bag kit (D). Inside you'll find a degradable waste bag (B) filled with a gritty powder (the decay catalyst). Go in this bag. Then pack the waste bag in the zip-close bag (A). The kits include (C) a small amount of toilet paper (in case you forget yours) and an antiseptic fresh nap for wiping your hands. Pack only waste in the kits (no food scraps or trash which might attract animals). Store used kits outside your tent. We prefer to carry them on the outside of a pack though you might safely devise a way to carry them inside your pack. Don't store them in a bear canister or any container to be used for carrying food. A disposal station is located near the outhouse at the Mt. Whitney Trail trailhead.

Keep water sources clean

A good rule of thumb is not to wash anything in any backcountry body of water. Carry all water for washing (sponge baths and dishes!) away from natural water sources in a collapsible bucket.

Wash hands away from all water sources before eating or preparing food. Use all soaps, even biodegradable ones, at least fifty feet from lakes and streams.

Mountain (Altitude) Sickness

Chances are, if you come up to climb Mt. Whitney from sea level, and aren't use to climbing above 8,000+ feet (though the symptoms of mountain sickness can start at any elevation), you should be prepared for possible discomfort–headache, nausea, dizziness, vomiting–all symptoms of mountain sickness (also called altitude sickness).

Altitude sickness is caused by reduced atmospheric pressure. This affects the body in two ways. One, it means that the body has a tougher time dredging oxygen out of the atmosphere, so, less oxygen for you. Two, small blood vessels actually leak fluid which can accumulate and press on the brain–hence, the headache. Medical mumbo jumbo aside there are several things you can do. As in everyday life, prevention is key.

Keep *hydrated* by drinking plenty of liquid with electrolyte and glucose replacement throughout the trip. Everyone has their individual preferences, but Gatorade and Gookinaid Hydrolyte are among the old standards. Dehydration greatly increases your risk of symptoms and reduces your body's physical and mental capabilities. In other words, you feel sicker and go slower. Because you're going slower, you're spending more time at altitude and therefore feel even sicker. Pretty much a bad deal all the way around.

The most important and surefire way to drastically reduce or even eliminate symptoms is to take some extra time to acclimatize. Depending on where you've just come from, spending an extra night at the trailhead would be a good idea. Whitney Portal, for example, is at 8,300 feet and has a large campground. The Eastern Sierra has many excellent day hikes that can provide valuable acclimatization before you begin your Whitney ascent.

Above: Cathy Reynolds and friend on the Tower Traverse. PHOTO: Murray Zichlinsky

Despite being in good physical shape, some people are just not able to acclimatize above certain elevations, no matter how much time they spend at elevation prior a trip or how much liquid they drink to keep hydrated. Those individuals may be candidates for the prescription drug, Diamox, which has been very effective in preventing altitude sickness at the highest elevations in the contiguous U.S. Diamox is taken in gradual doses of 125 or 250 mg. (up to 500 mg.) every 12 hours, three to four days before going to elevation.

On the following pages is a description for White Mountain Peak. A dayhike about half the distance and elevation gain of Mt. Whitney, White Mountain Peak is a great place to test your sensitivity to altitude.

On your hike or climb of Mt. Whitney don't be too eager to place your camp as high as possible. Long ago on a climbing trip to the Himalaya I learned of the dictum "Climb high, sleep low" from a more experienced team mate. Throughout that expedition and since then, this has proved to be sound advice. You stress your body by going high and then sleep low to enable the body to recover.

Keep hydrated by drinking water with electrolyte replacement while munching on energy snacks throughout the day. Carry an antacid for possible stomach nausea and acetaminophen for headaches (at altitude, acetaminophen is gentler on nauseated stomachs than conventional aspirin). Some people are just sensitive to elevation and no amount of water or food is going to keep them from getting sick. The key is to be able to judge how you handle high elevation before you commit to doing a trip with partners, and to do something about it so that you don't become a liability to your climbing partners or to yourself.

The air is much thinner at 14,000' than at sea level, so the lungs really get a workout. Over the years, we have noticed that smokers or people who have smoked heavily in the past, but who have quit,

Hiker on Russell-Carillon Pass PHOTO: Edward M. Zdon

tend to be affected by mountain sickness more often than people who have never smoked.

There are entire books written about mountain sickness by experts in the field of mountain or altitude sickness. Listed below are a few books for further reading on the subject:

High Altitude Illness and Wellness by Charles Houston, M.D.;
Mountain Sickness: Prevention, Recognition and Treatment by Peter Hackett, M.D.;
and *Mountain Medicine and Physiology: Proceedings of a Symposium for Mountaineers, Expedition Doctors and Physiologists, sponsored by the Alpine Club (London) edited by Charles Clarke, Michael Ward and Edward Williams.*

Third Highest Peak in California

Training for Altitude

White Mountain Peak (14,256 ft; 4,345 m)

Across the Owens Valley from Mt. Whitney is White Mountain Peak, one of two fourteeners in California *not* in the Sierra Nevada (the other being Mt. Shasta). The beauty about White Mountain Peak is that it can be done as a dayhike and is a great place to test your sensitivity to altitude.

The hike is about 14 miles round-trip with approximately 3,000 feet of elevation gain as compared to Whitney from the Portal, 22 miles round-trip with 6,000 feet of elevation gain. The hike to White Mountain's summit begins at a locked gate two miles south of the University of California's Barcroft Lab. Spending the night at the gate (no facilities) is highly recommended to acclimate and to get an early morning start. From the locked gate walk 2.0 miles on th well-worn dirt road to the lab, then another 5.0 miles on an old jeep track to the summit. The hiking is along the wide plateau of the crest, with excellent views of the Sierra. During the summer, marmots and migrating bluebirds are a common sight along the jeep trail, with bighorn sheep closer to the summit. A stone cabin that serves as a high altitude research facility tops the summit. Sometimes, the researchers are in there brewing up tea and have been known to offer a cup to tired summiteers. Naturally you'll then take a rest day or two. You are now in prime condition for Whitney.

Follow the road north past Barcroft and all the way to the summit of White Mountain. Since the starting point at the locked gate is just under 12,000' the high elevation is sustained the entire route.

White Mountain Peak PHOTO: Wynne Benti

Traditionally, the University of California held an open house at the lab on Labor Day, unlocking the gate for the day, cutting off four miles on the round-trip hike. Lately, they've been opening it up the first Sunday in August, so if you want to do the shorter hike, its best to call the White Mountain Research Station at (760) 873-4344 in advance to find out when they'll open the gate.

There is no water along the entire route. Carry at least 2-4 liters of fluid, as well as warm clothes and rain gear as thunderstorms tend to gather over the crest in the afternoon.

Bighorn sheep en route to White Mountain Peak PHOTO: Wynne Benti

Approach & Hiking Route

Maps: White Mountain Peak, Mount Barcroft and Juniper Mountain (CA) 7.5-minute (1:24,000 scale) topographic maps; Bishop 1:100,000 scale metric topographic map; Inyo National Forest Map; Automobile Club of Southern California (AAA) Eastern Sierra map

Best Time to Climb: June through October

Approach: From Westgard Pass, turn left on White Mountain Road (turns to dirt after 10.3 miles, just after Schulman Grove Visitor Center) 26.3 miles to a locked gate at a saddle between Piute Mountain and Mount Barcroft (11,650 ft). This approach is accessible to all cars.

Route: Pass the locked gate, and hike up the road about two miles to the Barcroft Laboratory at 12,400 feet. From the Barcroft Laboratory, continue to hike the road 5.5 miles to the summit. Anticipate about 14 miles and 3,000 feet of elevation gain round-trip.

(From "Desert Summits: A Climbing and Hiking Guide to Nevada and Southern California" by Andy Zdon, published by Spotted Dog Press)

Chapter Four

How to Get a Permit

Permits are required!

The most recent permit information including downloadable applications can be found on the Inyo National Forest website at:
http://www.fs.fed.us/r5/inyo/recreation/wild/whitneylottery.shtml
and by recorded message at (760) 876-6200. Anyone planning to hike Mt. Whitney by the main Mt. Whitney Trail during the peak (quota) season, May 1 to November 1, can reserve a permit early by submitting a *Mt. Whitney Lottery* application by mail, postmarked anytime during the month of February preceding the upcoming peak hiking season. The *Mt. Whitney Lottery* is the first opportunity to reserve a permit for any of the following: all overnight trips that start on the Mt. Whitney Trail; all day use hikes in the Mt. Whitney Zone via all routes; and for all day use hikes on the North Fork of Lone Pine Creek. Permits are not required for car camping in developed campgrounds.

When to apply

Applications for permits for the Mt. Whitney Lottery must be submitted by mail from February 1 through the last day in February. All applications must have a February postmark and all fees must accompany each application. Early applications are not accepted. No refunds are issued. Multiple applications that are submitted (to ensure a successful reservation) and accepted will not be entitled to refunds. On applications for dayhikes, the entry and exit date must be the day the you are hiking the trail.

On February 15, the USFS starts drawing applications at random and issuing reservations to the lucky winners who will be notified by mail. Results will be available by April 1st.

Where to apply

Applications for the Mt. Whitney Lottery may be downloaded off the Inyo National Forest website, or requested by mail or fax by calling the Wilderness Permit Office at (760) 873-2483. Applications are accepted by mail with a February postmark or proof of February pickup in the case of couriered mail. Faxed applications will not be accepted for the Mt. Whitney Lottery.

Mail applications to: Mt. Whitney Lottery, Wilderness Permit Office, 351 Pacu Lane, Suite 200, Bishop, CA 93514

Restrictions during peak (quota) season

A valid overnight or day use permit is required year-round (a limit or quota applies from May 1 to November 1) for all entry into the Mt. Whitney Zone. Permits are issued at the InterAgency Visitor Center in Lone Pine. Maximum group size is 15 people. All members of your party must enter the wilderness on the entry date specified on the permit. Only a listed alternate leader can replace the original leader if the group leader can't make the trip. A day use permit cannot be combined with an overnight trip and overnight permits cannot be used for dayhikes. Day use permits cannot be used on consecutive days; there must be one rest day between day hike attempts. Reservations will be canceled if the permit is not picked up or confirmed before the deadline: noon on the day before entry date for day use permits; 10 am on entry date for overnight permits.

To participate in the lottery, hikers and climbers must get an application from the USFS by phone, mail or fax, or download a Microsoft or Adobe PDF file from their website.

Lottery participation is not required for the following

It is not nececssary to apply for a permit during the lottery for overnight trips to Mt. Whitney that begin on another trail in the Inyo National Forest (i.e. Shepherd's Pass, Kearsarge Pass, North Fork of Lone Pine Creek/Mountaineer's Route, etc).

Participation in the Mt. Whitney Lottery is not required for hikes that do not enter the Mt. Whitney Zone or trips that begin in a National Park like Yosemite or Sequoia. Just specify the Mt. Whitney Trail as your exit and the permit issued by the National park will be valid for your entire trip including Mt. Whitney's summit and exit on the Mt. Whitney Trail). If you missed the February lottery you can apply for the few permits not reserved during the lottery process on a first come, first serve basis up until two days before the day of the trip.

To climb Mt. Whitney outside of the peak (quota) season, hikers and climbers may self-issue a permit at the Interagency Visitor Center in Lone Pine

Reservations and fees

For anyone entering the Mt. Whitney Zone, from any trailhead, a per person, per trip fee applies (check the Inyo National Forest website for current fees) regardless of the number of nights spent in the backcountry. This fee is separate from any pre-trip campground reservation fees. A check payable to the USDA Forest Service must be enclosed with the application. A confirmation letter is mailed to successful applicants with a receipt of payment and instructions for how to pick up the permit. Applications, including those paid with credit card numbers or checks will be returned to unsuccessful applicants within two months of the date submitted.

Processing fee

If you need to change the entry date or entry trailhead of your confirmed reservation, and quota space is available, there is a flat processing fee for the change. If space is available, additional party members can be added to an existing reservation and the same per person fees apply. Reservations cannot be sold or transferred.

Phone Reservations

Phone reservations are not accepted for the Mt. Whitney Lottery. Reservation requests for trips other than the Mt. Whitney Trail during peak season, are accepted on a rolling six-month basis (i.e., for trips starting July 1, applications are accepted beginning January 1). (760) 873-2483 is for reservations only. For information on campgrounds, trail conditions, etc., call the ranger station nearest to your trailhead. Since the reservation line can be extremely busy, faxing or mailing application are acceptable.

All reservations (mail, fax or phone) will be accepted up to two days before any planned entry. For example, if hikers plan to enter the wilderness on Friday, the USFS will stop taking reservations for that day at the close of business on Wednesday. If time does not allow the USFS to mail out a confirmation letter, they will provide information over the phone or fax a confirmation letter. If applying a week or less before a trip date, the USFS recommends that applications be made by fax or phone. Inyo National Forest Wilderness Permit Office, 351 Pacu Lane Suite 200, Bishop, CA 93514 Fax: (760) 873-2484; Wilderness Info: (760) 873-2485; General Recreation Information: (760) 873-2408; Reservation Line:(760) 873-2483 8am-4:30 pm, seven days a week from May 15–October 15; weekdays only the rest of the year

Walk-In-Permits

Any remaining walk-in permits, which are *free*, are available beginning at 11am on the day before your planned entry date. Mt Whitney and North Fork Lone Pine permits (and wag bags) can only be picked up at the InterAgency Visitor Center in Lone Pine. Any reserved permits not picked up by 10 am on the date of entry, are considered no-show permits and made available to other parties at 11am on a walk-in basis. Day hike no-show permits are available at 2pm, the afternoon before the hike. Demand for wilderness permits is high on weekends, holidays and during the months of July and August.

Chapter Five

Mt. Whitney in a Day

Preparation & Training

Climbing to the top of Mt. Whitney in a day is an incredible way to experience the peak. Starting out on a moonlit night the landscape is surreal and dream-like, the movement more of an inner voyage than an uphill trek. Then, on one of the many switchbacks you'll look over your shoulder and see the long strip of pumpkin orange lighting up the horizon over Death Valley. Within the next hour and a half you'll probably bear witness to some of the best alpenglow in the country, your whole world turning from cold blue shade to pink and then to warm orange as first the skyline, then the glacier carved cirques and finally the frosty alpine meadows come into crisp sunlit focus. At this point your psyche will be boosted to see how far you've come before most people have even eaten breakfast. Unburdened by a mule-ish overnight load, you get the full experience of night and day, from mooncast shadows in the boulder strewn pine forest right through to the achingly blue sky and and wide open summit plateau of the highest peak in the lower 48, concentrated into a single magical day you will always remember. As you crest the summit and look down the 10,000 foot escarpment to the valley floor you will know accomplishment with far greater dimensions than a marathon, feel euphoria more deeply than with any drug and experience the sky in a most elemental way.

Certainly there are benefits to spreading the ascent out over two or three days. From that first cup of coffee at an 11,000 foot camp to the slower pace and longer immersion into the alpine it is hard to argue with this, perhaps, more traditional type of approach. On the other hand, stepping lightly up the mountainside under a fraction of the load, the entire adventure, not just the summit, becomes the prized goal, an ongoing panorama of future memories. In more practical terms, on the Whitney Trail there are three times as many day permits available than overnight permits. And on the North Fork approach (to the Mountaineer's Route and the East Face routes) single day ascents do not require permits, thereby offering up an opportunity for spontaneity that is one of the most wonderfully unique aspects of mountaineering.

Just a few years ago these points were brought home to me when I went in to climb the East Face, a thousand foot 5.7 rock climb guarded by a steep and mostly trailless approach. This route was first climbed in 1931 by Norman Clyde, Glen Dawson, Jules Eichorn and Robert Underhill. From a high camp beneath the peak they climbed the intimidating rock wall, taking only 3.5 hours from the start of the difficulties to the summit. Having done the route before I wondered at the possibility of trying to equal their time, but this time starting at the car. Early one August morning I left Bishop and drove south to Whitney Portal. Leaving the parking lot at the first hint of dawn, I hoofed it up the trail to the North Fork cut-off, aiming to gain as much altitude as I could before the morning sun got hot. Pausing at the beginning of the climb to wait for a couple to finish the first pitch, I had a drink of water and then continued on to the top. Checking my watch on the summit, I was surprised to find it had taken me less than 2.5 hours, much better than I had hoped. This ascent taught me a couple of things. First, don't set your sights too low; you might surprise yourself. Second, I experienced no ill effects whatsoever from the altitude. By travelling lightly and quickly I simply didn't spend enough time at 13,000 and 14,000 feet to develop the initial symptoms of altitude sickness.

Travelling lightly has saved my skin more than once. A couple of years ago a friend and I day hiked up the North Fork en route to Mt. Russell, Whitney's next door neighbor to the north. At about 10,000 feet, as we crossed a wide granite slab, a large grouse charged out of a nearby willow bush. In a flash, the rooster sized bird flew up into our faces, freaking us out with its utter ferocity. As I spun away, it latched on to the back of my neck, its razor sharp beak just inches from my exposed carotid.

Mt. Whitney ILLUSTRATION: Dee Molenaar

Exploding into a manic Go-Go dance, I gyrated my way out of the grouse's clutches and ran like a bunny. Our narrow escape was only made possible by our light packs AND our adrenaline-fed terror.

Over the years I've spoken with many people who climbed Whitney or other big peaks in a single day, some of whom certainly do not look like athletes. From my own experience and in conversations with others I've found that, whether you're hiking up a trail or climbing a big wall in Yosemite, with proper preparation and streamlining one's load, the one day ascents actually feel easier than the two or three day ones.

Physical Training

It should be obvious that you will need to be physically fit enough before you pull into the trailhead parking lot. Wherever you live you probably have access to countryside or gyms that can help you get into good enough shape. *The keys to this are: regularity and consistency.* To be effective you must exercise at least twice a week and (if you're in lousy shape) keep it up for at least a couple of months. To stick with it, pick workouts that are fun–an hour or two hike up a hillside is often more enjoyable and certainly more to the point than running on flats.

Specificity. Make your workouts as sports specific as possible. Search out the best (and steepest) trails in your area. Contact local hiking clubs or mountain equipment stores if you need help. If you're stuck in a gym try the stairmaster or some similar apparatus. At first it will look and feel remarkably similar to a hamster wheel but once you get used to it you will still be able to get a great workout. The key is to simulate walking up a steep hill for a long time. For example, bicycling can get you very fit, but hiking up a steep hill can get you the right kind of fitness.

Variety. Mix up your workouts, both in length and intensity, for maximum effectiveness and to avoid getting stale. One day a week, try and go for a long day hike, preferably with a lot of elevation gain. In southern California, for instance, great hikes exist on Mt. Baldy, San Jacinto Peak, and Mt. Lukens, the highest point within Los Angeles city limits. In the San Francisco Bay area, Mt. Diablo and Mt. Tamalpais offer smaller, but still excellent hiking and hill running opportunities. If your handiest hills are small simply go for more intensity–go faster. The late, great mountaineer-photographer, Galen Rowell gained much of his legendary endurance running in the rather diminutive Berkeley Hills.

Sufficient Duration. An important concept is the pyramid–the broader the base, the higher the pyramid. This simply means that the more time and miles you put in early on, the fitter you can get and the further you can go. The earlier in the season you begin your training, the better. By slowly increasing your mileage over a longer period of time you decrease the chance of burnout and injury.

It is important to exercise aerobically for at least a half hour; forty five minutes is much better. Beyond one hour I see negligible benefits, except for your one day a week longer hike.

Rest. Make sure you get adequate rest between workouts. This is when your muscles actually get stronger. Make sure some of your runs or hikes are of only moderate intensity. If your legs feel stale it's fine to scale down or even eliminate that day's exercise. Remember, the worst thing you can do for your fitness is get injured.

My own springtime training for the High Sierra is pretty much a giant bell curve of fun. Living in Bishop, California, I hike and run a couple of the local trails three or four times a week. These are very steep and I seldom go more than an hour uphill. *(Note: running or hiking uphill has less impact on your joints than on flat terrain).* I then WALK downhill–this is very important. Running down gives next to no training benefit but offers a substantial risk of pounding the cartilage clean out of your knees and the not insignificant risk of landing on your face. When walking downhill I've gotten into the habit of never fully straightening and locking my knees. This bent-legged gait turns my legs into effective shock absorbers. As the season progresses and the snow line rises I try go for at least one four or five hour hike up into the foothills a week. By the time May rolls around I start bagging smaller peaks and easing off on the running and training hikes and then in June I more or less stop all "exercise" and concentrate exclusively on the fun part–all the stuff I've been dreaming about all winter.

Altitude: The final phase of preparation is relatively short, usually less than a week, but is every bit as important as getting strong legs and lungs. Although the objective is to climb Whitney in a day, the more days you can spend on this trip acclimatizing, the greater chance you'll have of not only succeeding but also of having fun and looking good while doing it (admit it, you do care) AND not throwing up on the summit.

Although many people coming up from sea level try to squeeze in the drive up, the acclimatization, the climb and the drive home into a weekend, I would advise against it. If this adventure is really important to you then try and take about a week. It will make all the difference.

Here is an example schedule that should work well:

Day One: Drive up and sleep at seven or eight thousand feet. The Mammoth area, while perhaps a bit out of the way, is a great place to cool out.

Day Two: Go for an easy day hike. There are a huge number to choose from. The increased circulation this exercise provides aids your acclimatization and is perfect antidote to sitting in a car for five or six hours. Sleep at nine or ten thousand feet. There are a lot of campsites this high between Tuolumne Meadows and the Bishop area. As well, there are a number of lodges that rent rooms or cabins.

Day Three: Minor exercise/relax. Spend another night at nine or ten thousand.

Day Four: Drive to Whitney Portal and sleep there.

Day Five: THE CLIMB!

Day Six: Drive home to the city (or call in sick and stay the summer)

Another great way is to acclimatize on another big mountain. My top choice for this would be White Mountain Peak, the highest peak in the White Mountains, just east of the Bishop area. The route description for White Mountain Peak as a dayhike is on pages 56-58.

A round-trip dayhike of White Mountain Peak is about 14 miles with 3,000 feet of gain compared to Whitney's 22 miles and 6,000 feet of gain. White Mountain is the third highest peak in California at 14,246-feet and is not only a perfect acclimatization peak but also a fine objective in its own right. Imagine reaching the highest points of two separate mountain ranges on one trip. Your bragging rights would be doubled.

To get there, go east from Big Pine on Highway 168, about thirteen miles and turn left on the White Mountain Road. Follow this paved road for ten miles to the Schulman Grove Visitor Center, well worth checking out. Just after this, the pavement ends and about twelve miles of good dirt road leads to a locked gate and the parking lot. Camping is allowed here but there are no facilities, apart from an outhouse. Spending the night here is highly recommended to acclimate and to get an early start. From the gate it is seven miles to the summit–two on a groomed dirt road and another five on an old jeep track. The hiking is mostly on the crest of a plateau-like ridge with excellent views of the Sierra. In the summer, there are marmots, bluebirds, and towards the top, bighorn sheep on occasion. The summit is capped by a stone cabin that is used as a high-altitude research facility by the University of California. If the summit is too cold and windy to enjoy, climb up the ladder to the tin roof like my friends and I did once. The metal roofing absorbs the sun's heat and provides a virtual skillet of a tanning deck.

Naturally you'll then take a rest day or two. You are now in prime condition for Whitney.

On the day of your climb, there are four crucial factors that, if paid attention to, will give you a much greater chance of success.

1. The Alpine Start

It is almost impossible to start too early. On the trail by three or four in the morning is about right although earlier allows even more time. Give yourself at least an hour from wakeup time at the Portal to your actual start time. It's surprising how much time gets eaten up by making coffee, packing and going number one and two. If your objective lies up the North Fork drainage leave no earlier than one hour before light as the route finding there gets too tricky in the dark. I made this mistake my first time in and ended up thrashing and cursing away in no man's land until sunrise.

2. Start Slow

This is no time to sprint out of the gate. The key is to start slower than you want to, to feel like you're holding back. Warming up slowly (for at least the first hour) will allow you to get the most out of your legs. Your best bet is to go slow until it gets light. There's plenty of things to trip you up and every time you do trip it beats you up that much more.

3. Drink Often

This cannot be stressed enough. Drink a lot the day before and on your climb day drink before you're thirsty. Carry two to three liters and bring either iodine pills or a filter to purify water from sources along the way. Use some kind of energy-electrolyte drink powder. The more expensive ones are actually a lot better (Cytomax is my favorite). I find they work best when mixed at half strength. Getting some sort of hydration system (CamelBak or similar system) is a great investment. These units have improved a lot over the years and allow you to sip regularly. They don't leak like they used to and they're easier to use. Don't put them in your pack upside down, though; it just doesn't work. I did this my first time using one and sucked like a starving vampire until I figured it out.

4. Snack Often

Every two hours or so have something light. Eating too much at one time makes you sluggish so go for small but regular snacks. Remember to take some "normal" food as well (like sandwiches) and don't just rely on energy bars or Gorp. Imagine if, at home, you went a whole day eating nothing but energy bars or Gorp. You'd be sickeningly reminded of childhood Halloween binges.

Gear: Keep it Lightweight

Since you're going for it in a day it's even more important to keep it light.

Headlamp: Make sure it's comfortable–it's going to be on your head for hours. Use a halogen bulb–they use batteries quicker but they're much brighter. Bring extra batteries, bulb, and a small LED flashlight or headlamp (for changing batteries or bulbs). This last point is especially important if you're hiking alone.

Note: Headlamps are much preferable to hand-held flashlights.

Shoes: A good pair of trail running shoes will work great for most people. Trail running shoes are more stable and a bit burlier than standard running shoes but still a lot lighter than hiking boots. If you have ankle problems wear boots but make sure that they actually support your ankles and don't just cover them. When choosing shoes keep in mind that a pound on your feet feels like five on your back. *Note: A good pair of socks (wool-synthetic blend) are a must. Bring an extra pair for the descent.*

Rain Gear: A lightweight rain jacket weighing less than a pound also doubles as a windbreaker. Big Gore-Tex units can easily weigh two or three times as much and take twice as much space in your pack. Rain pants are a bit more optional.

Pack: A hydration day pack with well-padded shoulder and waist straps. This should also have compression straps to keep the load close to your center of gravity.

Trekking Poles: A lot of people use them. They need to be adjustable and have built in shock absorbers. They do make hiking easier and certainly make one more stable but try them out before you go to Whitney–they take some getting used to.

Clothing: Use a layering system and dress in synthetics. Wool is OK but heavy.

Miscellaneous: Sun hat, sunblock, moleskin, breathable tape, and aspirin.

Pacing on the Climb

It's important that anyone you hike with is of approximately the same fitness and hiking speed. Trying to catch up OR slowing down to wait interrupts your optimum cruising speed and will tire you out far faster. Once you've warmed up and have found your cruising speed, keep to it. This is more important than keeping to a precise schedule. Know that you'll most likely experience ups and downs in your energy level, periods of fatigue where it feels very unlikely that you could possibly succeed and later on a returning swell of energy and even exhilaration. As you come into the last few miles and the altitude is kicking in, making even your light daypack feel heavy, keep plugging along and DON'T stash your pack (like I've seen a lot of people do). Now it is especially important to keep drinking and eating. As well, you'll most likely want your extra clothes on the summit and that pack may be surprisingly hard to find on the way down.

Enjoy your time on the summit but don't stay too long. The longer you stay the more the altitude will affect you. You've now got miles and miles to go to get back down, but don't worry. Gravity is on your side.

The Mt. Whitney Trail from Whitney Portal

Suggested hiking maps: Mount Whitney, CA and Mt. Langley, (CA) 7.5-minute (1:24,000 scale) USGS *topographic maps.*

The mileages on the Mt. Whitney Trail have been open to question. In preparation for the Mt. Whitney Marathon, Bob and Jerri Lee of Ridgecrest measured the distances from Whitney Portal to the summit, using a surveyor's tape. Their values are used here.

0.0 miles (8,361'): The trailhead is located just east of the Whitney Portal Store. A large wilderness display is located here, which is well worth studying. The trail starts immediately behind the display. The first half mile crosses treeless terrain and is often hot during summer months.

0.5 miles (8,480'): The trail enters John Muir Wilderness. Campfires are not allowed in the Whitney drainage. Carry portable backpacking stoves. The trail works back and forth, through dry high desert scrub and may be quite warm on a summer's day. Near the top of the brushy area, about two miles from the starting point, a couple of small springs are found running alongside the trail. Just before reaching the Lone Pine Lake junction, the trail fords the creek over a footbridge.

2.5 miles (9,420'): Lone Pine Lake Junction. The left branch leads over a small rise to this beautiful lake. The main trail continues straight ahead, up a dry, sandy streambed. A short series of switchbacks on the right wall crosses over a shoulder to Outpost Camp.

3.5 miles (10,365'): Outpost Camp. The trail may be submerged at the lower end of the meadow, but logs have been strategically placed to keep feet from getting wet. About mid-meadow the trail fords the stream. This is a good campsite, but is still a long way to the summit. Use the restrooms provided. A few more switchbacks, then another stream crossing and you arrive at Mirror Lake.

4.0 miles (10,640'): Mirror Lake. This is a nice picnic area, but filter the water. *Giardia lamblia* is a nasty parasite that makes an unexpected appearance now and then in unfiltered water from backcountry water sources. If you get *Giardia*, expect to be violently ill; even possibly vomiting up stomach lining and having to spend a night or two in the hospital, worst case scenario. Why take the chance? It is so easy to effectively remove the microscopic *Giardia* cysts from water with a portable water filter. Carrying all the liquid you need for a few days in a full pack, is unnecessary when a filter and two quarts is all that's needed. If you're dayhiking Mt. Whitney, you'll probably want to carry two quarts of liquid and a filter. Boiling water or treating it with purification tablets are additional options in the backcountry.

Just past Mirror Lake, the trail turns left and at the last stream crossing, is sometimes submerged. Follow the trail through the moist spots, then continue to your right.

5.0 miles (11,395'): Trailside Meadows. The trail now climbs to the right and continues up to a ridge, contouring over a bench to Trail Camp.

6.0 miles (12,039'): Trail Camp. This group of little ponds is the last sure water. On the north side of the larger pond is a sandy area with several large rocks. This area provides good campsites with some wind protection and is recommended for overnight camp. Use the restrooms provided. The next two miles, with its 97 switchbacks, leads to Trail Crest.

8.2 miles (13,000'): Trail Crest. This is where the summit ridge is crossed to the western slope. Here, the trail enters Sequoia National Park and remains in the park to the summit of Mt. Whitney. Dogs and firearms are not permitted past this point. The true Whitney Pass is about a mile south and is seldom used. From here the trail

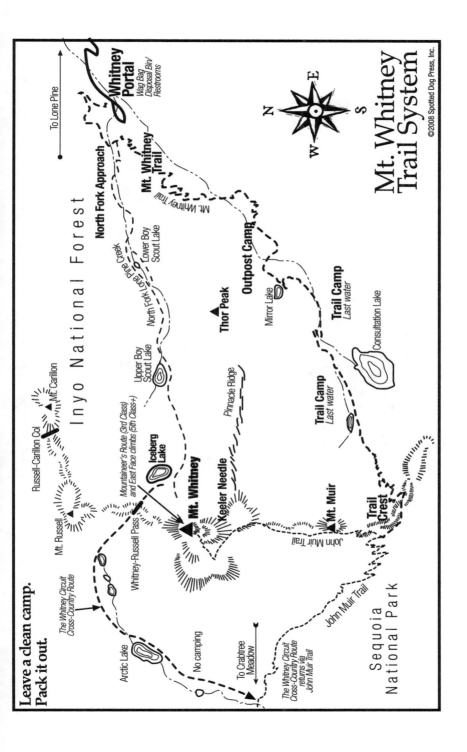

Mt. Whitney
Trail System

©2008 Spotted Dog Press, Inc.

Leave a clean camp.
Pack it out.

The summit register on Mt. Whitney PHOTO: Corinne Newton

drops slightly to meet the John Muir Trail.

8.7 miles (13,480'): The John Muir Trail. The route now passes the "'windows,'" with their spectacular view of the Owens Valley, then continues on up to the summit plateau. Follow the trail as it winds its way across a few more switchbacks, passing the stone shelter to the broad summit of Mt. Whitney.

10.7 miles (14,496'): You made it! The summit of Mt. Whitney. Sign the register in the historic summit shelter and enjoy the view.

Chapter Six

Other Trails & Cross Country Routes

The Long Way to Mt. Whitney

There are many routes to Mt. Whitney other than the main Whitney Trail and the North Fork, but most are arduously long multi-day backpacking trips (aka death marches) that still require a permit if you join up with or exit via the Mt. Whitney Trail.

Giant Forest

Perhaps the most popular alternate trip to Mt. Whitney is the Trans-Sierra jaunt from Giant Forest, completely across the Sierra Nevada, ending at Lone Pine. Often referred to as a one hundred mile hike, if a car shuttle can be arranged from the trail end to Lone Pine, the distance is about eighty miles. This trip is for experienced hikers with good physical endurance. A permit, available from the Lodgepole Visitor Center, is required for all overnight stays in Sequoia National Park. From Crescent Meadows, the High Sierra Trail hugs the 7,000-foot contour to Bearpaw Meadows (lodging and meals available during the season) where it continues on climbing past Hamilton Lakes with its spectacular view of Eagle Scout Peak and passes over the Kaweah Gap. It then descends the Big Arroyo to the Kern River. The trail swings north, leaving the river at Junction Meadow and joining the John Muir Trail at Wallace Creek. This is followed past Crabtree Meadow (last campsite below the peak), and joins the Mt. Whitney near Trail Crest, two miles south of the summit of Mt. Whitney. Use the bear boxes (BB) to store all food and scented items

Giant Forest to Mt. Whitney

BB = Bear Boxes	Elevation	Distance from point above	Distance from Crescent Meadow	Distance from Mt. Whitney	
Crescent Meadow	6,800'	0.0	0.0	68.5	BB
Bearpaw Meadow	7,760'	11.4	11.4	57.1	BB
Hamilton Lakes	8,235'	4.6	16.0	52.5	BB
Kaweah Gap	10,400'	5.5	21.5	47.0	
Upper Funston Mdw	6,720'	20.0	41.5	27.0	BB
Junction Meadow	8,036'	11.5	53.0	15.5	BB
Wallace Creek	10,400'	4.0	57.0	11.5	BB
Crabtree Meadow	10,329'	3.0	60.0	8.5	BB
Mt. Whitney	14,496'	8.5	68.5	0.0	

BB: Updated Bear Box information with GPS coordinates can be found online at www.climber. org

Mineral King to Mt. Whitney

From the alpine-like village of Mineral King several routes are available. The most popular leads over Franklin Pass, down Rattlesnake Creek, reaching the Kern River, a little south of the High Sierra Trail. From this junction, the route is the same as the above route. A much rougher but shorter route climbs directly east from Mineral King over Sawtooth Pass, dropping past Columbine Lake to the Big Arroyo. This trail is often in poor shape and is not recommended for pack stock. A third trail leads over Timber Gap, then cuts back and up over the hot, dusty Black Rock Pass and down again to the High Sierra Trail in the Big Arroyo.

	Elevation	Distance from point above	Distance from Mineral King	Distance from Mt. Whitney	
Mineral King	7,830'	0.0	0.0	52.1	
Franklin Lakes	10,240'	3.6	3.6	48.5	
Franklin Pass	11,680'	1.5	5.1	47.0	
Kern River	6,585'	16.0	21.1	31.0	BB
Upper Funston Mdw	6,720'	4.0	25.1	21.0	BB
Junction Meadow	8,036'	11.5	36.6	15.5	BB
Crabtree Meadow	10,329'	7.0	43.6	8.5	BB
Mt. Whitney	14,496'	8.5	52.1	0.0	

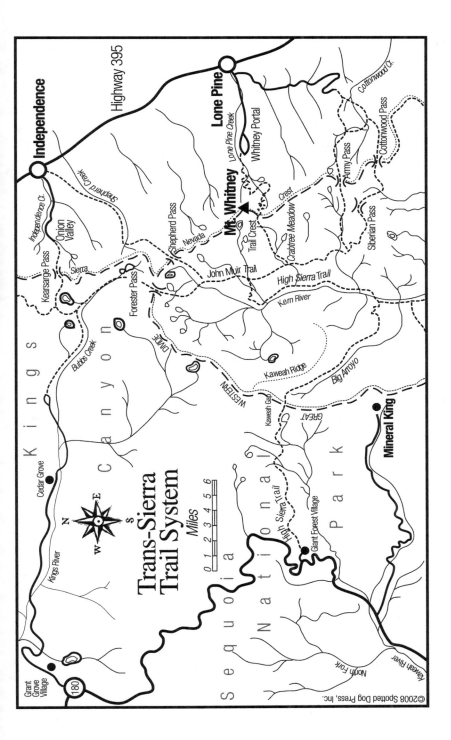

Trans-Sierra Trail System

Miles
0 1 2 3 4 5 6

©2008 Spotted Dog Press, Inc.

Cedar Grove to Mt. Whitney

A less commonly used route starts from the roadend above Cedar Grove in Kings Canyon and works its way up to Bubbs Creek, joining the John Muir Trail, just south of the trail junction from Kearsarge Pass. A loop trip can be arranged, returning to Giant Forest.

	Elevation	Distance from point above	Distance from Cedar Grove roadend	Distance from Mt. Whitney	
Roadend	4,855'	0.0	0.0	49.5	BB
Bubbs Creek	5,098'	5.0	5.0	44.5	BB
Junction Meadow	8,080'	9.5	14.5	35.0	BB
Vidette Meadow	9,600'	2.5	17.0	32.5	BB
Forester Pass	13,120'	7.0	24.0	25.5	
Wallace Creek	10,400'	10.0	34.0	15.5	BB
Crabtree Meadow	10,329'	7.0	41.0	8.5	BB
Mt. Whitney	14,496'	8.5	49.5	0.0	

Onion Valley to Mt. Whitney

Two longer trips may be taken from Onion Valley (9,120'), west of Independence, once home of California pioneer writer Mary Austin *(Land of Little Rain)*. It is about four miles to Kearsarge Pass from the beginning of the Onion Valley Trailhead. A short drop leads to Charlotte Lake (two BB), a suitable campsite (Bullfrog Lake is closed). This short climb over the pass is an excellent first day conditioner. From here the trail leads up over Forester Pass and joins the above route at Tyndall Creek Junction, but starts lower by some 3,000 feet.

	Elevation	Distance from point above	Distance from Onion Valley	Distance from Mt. Whitney	
Onion Valley	9,120'	0.0	0.0	35.7	BB
Kearsarge Pass	11,800'	4.0	4.0	31.7	
Bullfrog Lake	10,600'	2.0	6.0	29.7	CLOSED
Forester Pass	13,120'	8.2	14.2	21.5	
Tyndall Creek Junction	10,880'	5.0	19.2	16.5	
Wallace Creek	10,400'	5.0	24.2	11.5	BB
Crabtree Meadow	10,329'	3.0	27.2	8.5	BB
Mt. Whitney	14,496'	8.5	35.7	0.0	

Summit shelter on Mt. Whitney PHOTO: China Lake NAWS

Horseshoe Meadow to Mt. Whitney

Another less travelled route may be taken from the Horseshoe Meadow roadend up the Cottonwood Creek watershed, then over the New Army Pass to an intersection with the Pacific Crest Trail, which rims the Cottonwood Creek Basin, contouring from Mulkey Pass to Siberian Pass.

	Elevation	Distance from point above	Distance from Horseshoe Meadow roadend	Distance from Mt. Whitney	
Roadend	9,660'	0.0	0.0	30.7	BB
New Army Pass	12,385'	7.2	7.2	23.7	
Siberian Pass Trail	10,820'	7.0	14.2	16.5	
Crabtree Meadow	10,329'	8.0	22.2	8.5	BB
Mt. Whitney	14,496'	8.5	30.7	0.0	

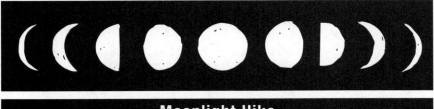

Moonlight Hike

A moonlight ascent of Mt. Whitney is a unique way to reach the summit. Essentially a dayhike at night, in years past, it was the last way to bypass the formal permit lottery process, but those days are long gone! The USFS now considers it an overnight trip and requires a permit. For those in shape enough to dayhike, or moonlight-hike Mt. Whitney, the views of the Eastern Sierra by moonlight, the coolness, lack of sunglare and people on the trail may make this a preferable way to hike the peak.

Choose an evening, just a night or two after a full moon (consult your calender). This will insure that the moonlight will illuminate the eastern slopes while you are hiking. The moon will then cross the crest with you and provide light on the western slope.

Sierra nights can be cold, especially with a brisk wind. Carry a parka, sweater, a warm wool hat and warm gloves. A lightweight bivy sack, can make any evening on Whitney's summit all the more enjoyable. If you reach the summit before sunrise, the wait can be cold. Carry a flashlight or headlamp (you may not need it with the moonlight), lunch, trail snacks and at least two quarts of water. Photographs taken at sunrise, with the sun casting its peach and pink glow across the Sierra Crest as it rises over the White Mountains to the east, can be spectacular.

Before 12:00 midnight, an overnight permit is required for all moonlight hikes, with or without camping. If you enter at 12:01am and are out by midnight the next day, then it is considered a dayhike. Park in the overnight parking area.

The Whitney Circuit: A Peter Croft Classic

This beautiful cross-country route begins by ascending the cliff-lined North Fork drainage up past the east facing walls of Mt. Whitney. It then crosses the Sierra crest just to the north, descends past the Arctic Lakes to Guitar Lake and circles back up the peak's west side on the John Muir Trail. In addition to travelling through the most spectacular terrain in the area, this route also offers the mountaineer a chance to climb routes on the east side of Whitney and the south side of Mt. Russell. *(Note: See climbing section for description on routes)*

There are a few ways to make this grand, cross-country tour of Mt. Whitney:

1. The first uses the main Mt. Whitney Trail as the descent.

2. The second uses the Mountaineer's Route and North Fork drainage as the descent.

3. The third uses the Mountaineer's Route to the summit, then follows the trail down to Trail Crest and turns west on the John Muir Trail to Guitar Lake. It leaves the trail here and hikes up past the Arctic Lakes to the Whitney/Russell Col and the North Fork drainage.

4. A fourth option involves leaving the North Fork drainage at Upper Boy Scout Lake and heading up to the East Arete of Mt. Russell. Climb this and descend the South Face Route to the Arctic Lakes drainage.

The advantage of the first option is that you don't double back on hardly any of the approach.

The advantage of the other two options is that you'll only be on the busy Whitney Trail for two miles. (In my opinion this makes for a superior trek.) For the rest of the time you'll have the place much more to yourself.

Corinne Newton on the Mountaineer's Route with the Arctic Lakes below   PHOTO: Justin Schmunk

Follow the approach to the south face of Mt. Russell. Once over the Whitney-Russell Col simply follow the obvious drainage down past the Arctic Lakes. After the initial talus beneath the col, the rest of the way down past these beautiful lakes is an easy and enjoyable 2.0 miles to Guitar Lake. Turn left on the John Muir Trail and follow this for 3.5 panoramic miles to Trail Crest. Turn left again at this trail intersection and ascend the last 2.0 miles on the Whitney Trail to the summit.

Descend either the Whitney Trail or the Mountaineer's Route (and North Fork drainage.)

Hiking with Dogs

We love our canine friends, however, *they are not permitted* on the trails or in the back-country of Sequoia or Kings Canyon National Parks, or on the summit of Mt. Whitney which is on the border of Sequoia National Park and Inyo National Forest. From the Mt. Whitney Trail, the cutoff for canines is at Trail Crest—*no dogs allowed past this point.*

There are plenty of places dogs are allowed, including most BLM, USFS lands (with the exception of certain research areas, such as the Bighorn Sheep Zoological Area near Mt. Williamson, and any other areas that may be designated off-limits for archeological or environmental reasons), and most USFS wilderness areas. Dogs are not allowed in the backcountry of U.S. national parks, nor are they permitted in the backcountry or on the trails in California state parks, though this rule sometimes varies. Dogs are allowed on leash in Bodie State Historic Site, but they are not allowed in San Jacinto State Park near Palm Springs. It is always best to check ahead with the managing park agency before traveling many miles with your dog, only to find out that canines are not allowed beyond the parking lot.

Here's a true story about a fellow who lost his dog, Mandy, up the North Fork of Big Pine Canyon in the Sierra. Unleashed and wearing a dogpack, she wandered off into the backcountry and was unable to find her way back to her owner despite his calling and looking for her for several hours.

For two weeks, Mandy's owner returned to the area to look for her. He notified local animal control, posted reward ads in the local newspaper and signs in local neighborhoods, until business took him to Hong Kong. Nearly a month had passed, with no

Dogs are not allowed past Trail Crest or in the backcountry of the National Parks
PHOTO: Wynne Benti

word of Mandy.

Then, one morning about a month later, in the town of Big Pine, a resident walked out into her backyard, where she found an emaciated and very dehydrated dog playing with her own dog. It was Mandy. Though she had lost her pack and endured the backcountry for almost a month, she made it back to civilization, without being torn to shreds by mountain lions or coyotes, or being shot. This dog and owner were happily reunited, but others have not been so lucky.

Nancy Smith, Inyo County Animal Control Officer and Inyo County Search and Rescue team member, recommends that owners keep their dog leashed while hiking in the Sierra, especially if the dog is going to carry its own pack. There have been cases where dogs have gotten away from their owners while carrying packs, and have been found drowned in streams or hanging dead on trees or snags, unable to escape, strangled by their own collars. *A dog off-leash can become very easily disoriented in the backcountry.* Dogs that know only a home aren't trained in backcountry survival. They can't read maps or trail signs or navigate by the sun.

Here are a few other good reasons to keep dogs leashed: fast-moving stream crossings, pack animals; range cattle; disturbance of native wildlife; mountain lions and coyotes who see domestic dogs as a food source; children and people who are afraid of dogs; and people who don't just like dogs. Carry a leash with you at all times, and make sure your dog has an ID on its collar or a microchip surgically inserted in its neck. By keeping your dog leashed and close to you, you can assure your pet's safety and happiness.

Chapter Seven

Technical Routes

Mt. Whitney and Mt. Russell

Rating the Climbs

All of the technical climbing routes in this book are rock climbs so the only rating system needed refers specifically to rock routes. Obviously in stormy and/or winter conditions snow and ice can drastically change the whole character of the routes. In these conditions only very advanced climbers need apply and this type of winter climbing lies beyond the scope of this book. In normal conditions these climbs are enjoyable routes on good granite where the thin air of high altitude is much more of a concern than snow and ice.

The standard system for rating rock climbs is the Yosemite Decimal System, a general guide used to determine just the technical difficulty of a given climb. It does not take into account things like the altitude or afternoon thundershowers. As well, it does not take into account the wild exposure that you'll find on these routes or the fact that climbing with a pack makes you feel like you've packed on some poundage over the holidays and that you're climbing like a chubby boy.

The system works like this:

Class 1: Trail hiking. The main Mt. Whitney Trail is Class 1.

Class 2: Rough, off-trail or cross country hiking. Hands may be occasionally needed for balance. The North Fork Approach is an example of Class 2.

Class 3: Steeper terrain where hands will be needed for balance and climbing. Climbing is easy but there is increased exposure and therefore a substantial risk of injury or worse in the event of a fall. Some people may want a rope although most people won't need one. The Mountaineer's Route on Mt. Whitney is an example of a Class 3 route although there is only a short section of that difficulty. The East Arete of Mt. Russell is an excellent example of a sustained Class 3 climb.

Class 4: Generally steeper terrain where most people will want a rope. The terrain is trickier and there is usually greater exposure. Some people will want to stop and belay. Many people, however, will move together a rope-length apart, the leader placing gear and the second taking it out. This is often called fourth classing or simu-climbing and is a faster way to climb this kind of terrain while still being attached to the mountain. There are a number of Class 4 sections on the East Face and East Buttress routes.

Class 5: Climbing becomes more difficult and most climbers will want to place protection and stop to belay at regular intervals. Class 5 is subdivided from 5.0, 5.1, 5.2 etc. to (at present) 5.15. From 5.10 and upwards the grades are further subdivided into a,b,c and d. For example 5.10a would be easier than 5.10c. The East Buttress of Mt. Whitney and the Fishhook Arete on Mt. Russell are examples of Class 5 routes.

The Roman Numeral System (overall grade) is from I to VI:

I: up to a few hours
II: about half a day
III: an easy to moderate day
IV: a full day
V: a day and a half to two days
VI: more than two days

These grades are for the average climber and are meant to describe the time and effort from the base of the route to the summit. The approach to the base of the climb adds more time.

Climbing Equipment

Bring comfortable climbing shoes, not tight-fitting gym slippers. I use a stiffer, board-lasted shoe that supports and protects my entire foot. Since the chances of doing any hanging belays are slim to none on the broken up ledges of the mountain rock, a lightweight harness will work. Use a 9 mm rope for the moderate routes (you can always double up and do short pitches if things start looking nasty) and a 9.5 to 10 mm, 60 meter rope, for the harder routes.

I recommend using an *alpine rack* for the easier less sustained mountaineering routes and a *technical rack* for the more serious, continuous climbs. An *alpine rack* should include a half dozen stoppers, a few cams, a half dozen slings, and a cordelette or two along with ten or twelve carabiners. A *technical rack* for Sierra climbs is different than a rack used for Yosemite or Joshua Tree in that you'll need about ten extra slings, and a couple of cordelettes. Some of the slings should be knotted so you can untie and thread them around an anchor for a rappel. The cordelettes, apart from their usual uses for equalizing anchors, can be looped over gigantic boulders or small pinnacles. Other gear should include a set of stoppers and a set of cams from 1/2" to 3". Some folks prefer using hexes which are a better alternative if you have to leave them behind as rappel anchors. Otherwise the multidirectional function of the camming units and their ability, especially in the larger sizes to fit a large array of crack widths makes it possible to carry less weight. On routes that need other specific gear or a lot of one size, such gear will be so noted on the route maps. There are offwidths on Keeler Needle however, Warren Harding put in a string of bolts beside them so there is no need to carry head-sized cams up there.

For first aid, I bring a handfull of aspirin (altitude headaches), and a roll of breathable tape for bandaging cuts as well as repairing frayed trigger cables, camming devices, broken headlamps. For unplanned overnight stays, carry a lightweight bivy sack and some matches for making a fire (under 11,000').

Heading to the Mountaineer's Route PHOTO: Corinne Newton

Mt. Whitney Vicinity

The North Fork Approach

The North Fork of Lone Pine Creek is the approach used for all technical climbs listed in this book.

From Whitney Portal follow the Whitney Trail past a small stream at 0.5 mile to a bigger stream at about 0.65 of a mile. Take the small, steep trail to your right on the north side of the creek (just before the main Mt. Whitney Trail crosses the creek).

A shortcut to this point takes the old, unmaintained trail at the west end of the highest parking area beginning behind some big boulders. Follow this as it switchbacks steeply up to the main Mt. Whitney Trail, turn right (downhill) and walk a hundred yards or so to the North Fork of Lone Pine Creek. Cross this on stepping stones and take an immediate left onto the North Fork Trail.

The trail is easy to follow at first. After 0.5 mile it crosses to the south side of the creek, continues up that side for another 0.5 mile and then crosses back to the north side where it butts up against a cliff. After a short distance a small chute appears in the cliff to your right just beneath a large pine tree. Easy scrambling up this chute leads out of the main drainage and onto some sidewalk-sized ledges that head east for a hundred feet or so before allowing access to a forested area where the route leads back west (towards Whitney). Some of this section is quite exposed.

The steep and scrappy trail stays on the right side of the creek up a brushy hillside to Lower Boy Scout Lake, a pretty spot to camp. From here there are two options. The first crosses the creek at the lake's outlet and follows the lake's south shore a few hundred yards before heading up a steep talus field. Bits and pieces of trail head up this and then traverse right through a brushy area to smooth granite slabs beside the creek. Cross the creek to the right side and find easier going on the trail heading to Upper Boy Scout Lake, an even better place to camp.

The other option (faster and clear of snow earlier) leaves Lower Boy Scout Lake half way along its north (right) side and heads for a gully (with a couple of big pine trees in it) on the right side of an obvious giant slab just up and west of the lake. Go a short distance up this gully before cutting out left onto the slab. It was at this point just a few years ago that I received a sound bitch-slapping from an angry grouse. Although roughly the size and shape of a large chicken this enraged piece of poultry was clearly gaining the upper hand before I was able to break free and run. Be warned! Angle up left to the top of the slab where forested slopes allow you to contour left a short distance to open flat granite slabs that are followed uphill to join up with the trail just below Upper Boy Scout Lake.

If Mt. Russell's East Ridge is on your agenda, hike (grovel) up sandy scree slopes above the lake's outlet to the north, gaining 1,400 feet of elevation until you arrive at a sloping plateau. Hike easily northwest up this to the obvious col between Mt. Carillon on the right and Mt. Russell on the left. Russell's East Ridge is the obvious left skyline.

The approach to Iceberg Lake and Whitney's East Face routes goes south from the lake's outlet a 0.3 mile or so before swinging west and continuing for another mile. If headed for Keeler, branch off left just before here and make your way to its base. Look for an area of black water streaks on the cliffs to your right. It's possible to ascend just left of these streaks but it's better to continue another few hundred feet west to an easier way through the cliff band. Just above lies Iceberg Lake, the highest place you might want to camp. The nights are especially cold here and the rocky terrain is barren of trees and grass. The scene is awesomely spectacular, though, your tent crouched beneath the dominating granite shield of Whitney's east face and flanked by the fiercely blue Iceberg Lake.

To reach the East Face and East Buttress Routes start from the south end of the lake and hike and scramble straight up bluffy but easy terrain left of the obvious scree filled couloir (the Mountaineer's

Heading up the Ebersbacher Ledges on the North Fork Approach PHOTO: Corinne Newton

Route) to reach a notch between two towers. This is the rope up spot. To reach the Mountaineer's Route aim for the broad couloir. To reach the Whitney-Russell Col (as for Russell's South Face routes and the Whitney Circuit) walk round the left side of the lake to the far end and then start aiming up and left for a high notch in the ridge. *Note: The Whitney-Russell Col is also known as the Whitney-Russell Pass.*

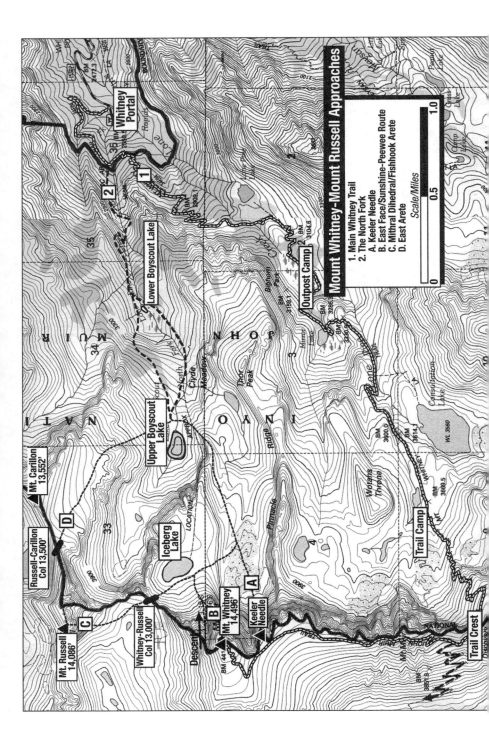

Mount Whitney-Mount Russell Approaches

1. Main Whitney Trail
2. The North Fork
   A. Keeler Needle
   B. East Face/Sunshine-Peewee Route
   C. Mithral Dihedral/Fishhook Arete
   D. East Arete

Scale/Miles

0   0.5   1.0

Whitney Portal

Lower Boyscout Lake

Outpost Camp

Upper Boyscout Lake

Iceberg Lake

Clyde Meadow

Thor Peak

Bighorn Park

Mirror Lake

Pinnacle Ridge

Wotans Throne

Trail Camp

Consultation Lake

Trail Crest

Mt. Carillon 13,552'

Russell-Carillon Col 13,500'

Mt. Russell 14,086'

Whitney-Russell Col 13,000'

Descent

Mt. Whitney 14,496'

Keeler Needle

INYO NATIONAL

JOHN MUIR

BM 14,418

NATIONAL

MT. WHITNEY TRAIL

BM 3868.5

Mt. Whitney Vicinity

Keeler Needle V 5.10c

First Ascent: Warren Harding, Glen Denny, Rob McKnight and Desert Frank, July 1960
First Free Ascent: Chris Vandiver, Galen Rowell, and Gordon Wiltsie, August 1976
Approach Mileage and Elevation gain: 5.0 miles–1.0 mile on good trail, 3.0 mile on mostly good cross country. The last mile on rough talus and moraine. 4,800 feet of gain.
Total Gain: 6,200 feet
Area Map: Page: 94
Topo of Route: Page 96
Photo: Page 97

Keeler's first ascent back in 1960 was an important one that helped point the way to the many big wall opportunities throughout the High Sierra. its first free ascent was also an important one, for it helped show the free climbing possibilities on big alpine walls. its first solo ascent, however, was something altogether different.

One summer in the late 1980s, Walt Shipley, reeling from a romantic blowout, fled to Keeler in hopes of purging his soul. After camping near its base he arose to discover that a cold storm had swept through, dusting the face with snow. His decision to continue on regardless might be seen as a simple suicide mission but Walt, although crazed, had broad experience with big bold solos. This desperate but successful climb was especially impressive for the painstaking care that was needed to clear snow off finger and foot holds, stretching out this historic ascent and providing a nail biting testament to Walt's cool.

The Approach: See pages 91-93 (The North Fork Approach)
The Climb: Start at the left side of the face and climb up and

Opposite: Derived from Mt. Whitney and Mt. Langley, CA USGS 7.5 minute topos (Scale: 1:24 000)

Keeler Needle - V 5.10c

Gear List:
Technical rack plus
extra 2″ to 4″ and a 5″ piece

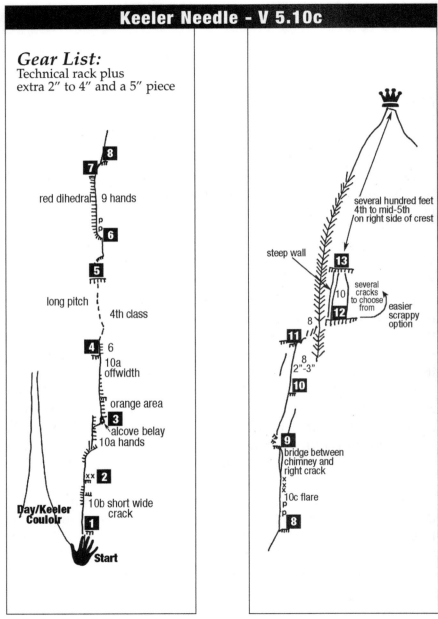

All drawings: Peter Croft

Keeler Needle – V 5.10c PHOTO: Peter Croft

slightly right on slabby cracks to a ledge about 50 feet up. Up the main crackline, climbing a wide crack through a roof (5.10 loose flakes in back of crack) and belaying 40 feet higher at two bolts. Follow the main crackline above through another overhang on bottoming handcracks and then exit right out of the corner via a face crack to an alcove belay beneath an area of orange rock. Climb the corner above which turns to off width (5.10). A couple hundred feet of easy climbing leads to a ledgy area. Go up and right into a crack which ends at a sloping ledge beneath the right facing Red Dihedral. Climb this fun pitch (5.9, some fixed pins) to a ledge. An easy short pitch leads to the crux wide crack. Up this (5.10c, some fixed gear) to a belay on the left. Go up and right for a couple of pitches to a ledgy area. 5.8 flakes go up and right around the corner to a big ledge on the prow with steep wall above lined with several cracks. The cleanest and best looking one is fun 5.10 finger and hand jamming. You can also weasel around to the right on 5.8 ground to avoid the steep wall before heading back up towards the crest. Stay just right of the crest for several hundred feet of class 4 to the summit.

The Descent: Drop down to the main Mt. Whitney Trail and take that to Whitney's summit. From there follow the East Face descent route (the Mountaineer's Route)

Mt. Whitney

East Face III 5.7

First Ascent: Glen Dawson, Jules Eichorn, Norman Clyde and Robert Underhill, August 16, 1931.

Approach Mileage and Elevation Gain: 5.0 miles–1.0 mile on good trail, 4.0 mile on a mostly good cross country route. 5,200 feet of elevation gain.

Total Gain: 6,200 feet

Area Map: Page 94

Topo of Route: Page 101

Photos: Page 100, 102-103

    This is my favorite route up Mt. Whitney for a number of reasons. The approach is comparatively short and steep but action packed with constantly changing mountain scenery and a fraction of the crowds that often mob the main Mt. Whitney Trail. The climbing on the face itself is instantly spectacular as you step out of the starting notch into the mid-air exposure of the first pitch. The rock is solid, the difficulties surprisingly straightforward and as you gain height, the wandering nature of the route creates the best bird's eye views of the eastern escarpment.

    The Approach: See pages 91-93 (The North Fork Approach)

    The Climb: Once the notch between the First and Second Towers has been gained the route angles out left across the south face of the Second (upper) Tower to a short chimney and exits onto the base of a lower angled area called the Washboard. Climb this easier section for a few hundred feet to where the rock steepens up and then angle up and left to a small notch, then continue around the corner, dropping down a bit to a large ledge near the base of some steep cracks. Instead of climbing these cracks (they're a more difficult variation) angle up and left for about 30 feet across the well named Fresh Air Traverse, a series of airy shelves with a few fixed pitons

Mt. Whitney
A. East Face
B. East Buttress aka
   Peewee Route

Descent
Mountaineer's Route

Descent

A

B

First
Tower

Second
Tower

PHOTO: Andy Selters

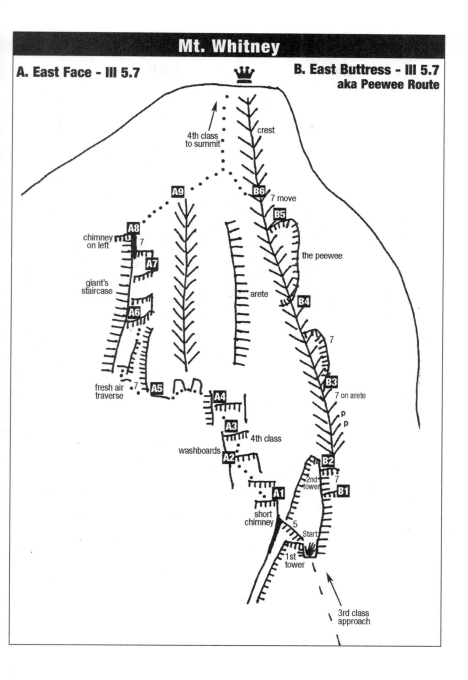

Mt. Whitney

A. East Face - III 5.7

B. East Buttress - III 5.7
aka Peewee Route

crest

4th class to summit

A9

B6 7 move

B5

chimney on left   7

the peewee

A8

A7

giant's staircase

arete

A6

B4

7

fresh air traverse   7   A5

A4

B3

7 on arete

A3

4th class

washboards   A2

p
p

B2

2nd tower   7

A1

B1

short chimney   5   Start

1st tower

3rd class approach

Mt. Whitney
A. East Face
B. East Buttress
C. Mountaineer's Route

East Buttress (direct route)

Grand Staircase

Mountaineer's Route

A

B

The Washboard

C

Mt. Whitney
A. East Face
B. East Buttress
C. Mountaineer's Route

A

Grand Staircase

B

Peewee

Fresh Air
Traverse

East Buttress

C

The Washboard

Second Tower

East Face Route

First Tower

Mountaineer's Route

Starting up the Washboard PHOTO: Murray Zichinlsky

for protection. This leads to cracks and chimneys that are climbed up to the Giant Staircase, a series of rubbly ledges about eight feet apart. Ascend these easily for a few hundred feet to where the ledges end and then climb a short chimney on the left. The angle eases off now and the route goes up and right to ledgier and easier terrain that leads straight up to the summit.

The Descent: Walk west on the summit plateau for a few hundred feet and descend the Mountaineer's Route down the north side of the peak. This is fairly easy scrambling (if conditions aren't snowy or icy) down blocky and then ledgy terrain to a large notch. Turn right (east) at the notch and descend the very obvious broad gully back down to Iceberg Lake.

Note: If conditions in the gully are bad (e.g. soft, sloppy snow or tedious talus) easier going can be found on the low angled rib of rock halfway down on the right side of the gully.

Mt. Whitney

East Buttress III 5.7 aka Peewee Route

First Ascent: Glen Dawson, Richard Jones, Muir Dawson, Bob Brinton and Howard Koster, September 5, 1937
Approach Mileage and Elevation Gain: 5.0 miles–1.0 mile on good trail, 4.0 mile on a mostly good cross country route. 5,200 feet of gain.
Total Gain: 6,200 feet
Area Map: Page 94
Topo of Route: Page 101
Photos: Page 102-103
　　This fine sister route to the East Face (they both start in the same place) was the second route to climb the huge cliffs above Iceberg Lake. Once again the young and talented Glen Dawson was on the first ascent and for good reason, too. On his ascent of the East Face route he had hungrily eyed the beautiful buttress just to the right. Six years later he went back and plucked this second plum. Glen was one of the very best rock climbers in the country and in that very same year he and Richard Jones made the first ascent of the scary Mechanic's Route on southern California's Tahquitz Rock, perhaps the hardest rock climb in the country at the time. I've repeated this and a number of his other routes in the high Sierra and have always come away impressed and often actually awestruck, considering their equipment of the day–hemp rope and basketball boots–Yikes!
　　The Approach: See pages 91-93 (The North Fork Approach)
　　The Climb: Once the notch between the First and Second Tower has been gained, an obvious left facing corner will be seen just to the right on the east face of the Second Tower. Climb this until you're about fifteen feet from its top and then traverse around to the right to a notch. From here, delicate face climbing (5.7, fixed pitons)

Mountaineer's Route PHOTO: Corinne Newton

leads straight up the crest. Climb the right facing corner above and continue up the buttress for a few hundred feet, avoiding difficulties on the right until you reach Peewee, a massive protruding block. Pass this on its right side and then climb up and slightly left to a short right facing corner (5.7 move). Angle up and left on easier and blockier climbing that leads to the summit.

Descent: Same as the East Face.

Mt. Whitney

Mountaineer's Route ~ Class 3

First Ascent: John Muir, October 21, 1873
Approach Mileage and Elevation Gain: 5.0 miles–1.0 mile on good trail, 4.0 miles on a mostly good cross-country route. 5,200 feet of gain.
Total Gain: 6,200 feet
Area Map: Page 94
Photo: Page 100 (shown as descent route), 102-103

John Muir climbed this route in 1873, only a couple months after the mountain's first ascent, a bold undertaking considering how fearsomely steep the climb appeared and the fact that he was alone. But the man was quite used to solo ventures and as it turned out the difficulties were quite short and moderate.

In good firm snow conditions this is an incredibly enjoyable and scenic ascent. On the other hand, in poor conditions (no snow) it can be a slidey talus treadmill or (in soft snow) a wallowing, slippery pig crawl to the top of the main gully.

The Approach: See pages 91-93 (The North Fork Approach)

The Climb: From Iceberg Lake aim for the obvious gully just right of the East Buttress. In soft snow or talus conditions it's easier to keep to the left side of this gully on easy ledgy terrain until that runs out and easy terrain is visible on the right side. Aim for this and continue to a high notch. Descend a little bit to the west and then turn left and go up a Class 3 shallow troughy area (hardest part at the bottom) to the summit plateau.

Descent: Descend the same route.

Mt. Russell

Mt. Russell (14,086 ft; 4,293 m)

This is considered one of the finest peaks in the entire Whitney area. Good granite, no easy way up and a tiny fraction of the crowds on Mt. Whitney (just one mile to the south) make this, in fact, one of the best high peaks in the entire range. Many routes climb its flanks, but three stand out as remarkable.

Above: South Face and East Arete (pages 115-116) of Mt. Russell PHOTO: Marty Lewis

Mt. Russell
A. Mithral Dihedral
B. Fishhook Arete
C. East Arete

East Summit

West Summit

Descent

Descent

C

B

A

PHOTO: John Moynier

Mt. Russell

Mithral Dihedral III 5.10a

First Ascent: Alan Bartlett and Alan Roberts, July 1976
Approach Mileage and Elevation Gain: Same as for Fishhook Arete
Total Gain: 6,100 feet
Area Map: Page 94
Topo of Route: Page 111
Photo: Page 112

As you approach the south face of Russell, this huge left facing corner is hard to miss. The first couple of pitches may be pretty scrappy and the last three or four may be typical High Sierra granite, however that central dihedral is quite unique. Three hundred feet of steep hand-jamming, devoid of ledges. The continuity of the climbing (and your obscene breathing) quickly makes you aware that you're approaching 14,000 feet.

The Approach: Same as Fishhook Arete

The Climb: There are a couple of minor corners leading up to the main one. Take the left hand of these and angle up this for a couple of fairly cruddy pitches (5.7 and 5.8+) to a small belay ledge at the base of The Corner. Huff and puff for two pitches of burly hand cracks ending at an incredible ledge out right on the prow. *(Note: charisma points will automatically be docked for those breaking this section into more than two pitches.)* Easier climbing leads 40 feet up to another ledge and then continue up blocky steps (turning most difficulties on the left) several hundred feet to the summit.

Descent: Same as Fishhook Arete

Mithral Dihedral III 5.10a

Gear List:
Technical rack plus
triples of cams 1.5" to 2.5"

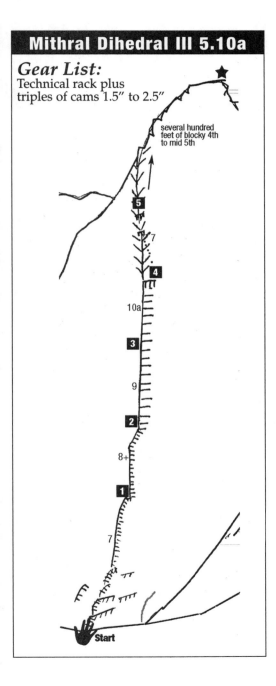

several hundred
feet of blocky 4th
to mid 5th

5

7

4

10a

3

9

2

8+

1

7

Start

Mithral Dihedral PHOTO: Dan Patitucci/Patitucci Photo

Mt. Russell

Fishhook Arete III 5.8

First Ascent: Gary Colliver and John Cleare, June 1974
Approach Mileage and Elevation Gain: 6.0 miles–1.0 mile on good trail, 5.0 miles on mostly good cross-country. 5,300 feet of gain.
Total Gain: 6,100 feet
Area Map: Page 94
Photo: Page 109, 114

This is the best alpine rock climb in the entire Whitney region. The rock is excellent all the way to the summit and the climbing is brilliantly varied and sustained right up the crest of this granite dragon's back.

The Approach: Follow the approach on page 92-93 to the Whitney-Russell Col. From there walk easily down and over to Russell's South Face. The Fishhook is the beautiful sweeping arete just right of the giant left facing corner of the Mithral Dihedral.

The Climb: Gain the arete near its base and climb easily up to a bulging headwall about a hundred feet up. Avoid this by climbing up and right onto the east (right) side of the arete on knobby flakes and regain the crest just above. Continue up, skirting any difficulties just left of the actual crest until you reach a notch. From here just climb straight up the arete to the summit. So much fun!

Descent: If you don't have gear left at the base and don't have to go back via Iceberg Lake, the East Arete is the most classic descent. Otherwise go east along the East Arete until you're about a hundred west of the East Summit. Look for a chimney corner system (Class 3) that drops down to the south for 70 or 80 feet to a scree slope. Follow the sand and talus back down. *(Note: The East Arete, page 116, is the easiest route up Mt. Russell.)*

Mt. Russell
A. Mithral Dihedral
B. Fishhook Arete

Descent

A

B

PHOTO: Andy Selters

Mt. Russell

South Face ~ Right Side Class 3

First Ascent: A.E. Gunther, 1928
Approach Mileage: 6.0 miles
Total Elevation Gain: 6,100 feet
Area Map: Page 94
Photo: Page 108-109

This route was the second climb done on Mt. Russell. It follows the easiest line on the peak up a swath of talus and sand to a short Class 3 headwall. The sandy talus is tedious and breath taking in the literal sense but the 80-foot headwall plops you on top of the summit ridge only a couple hundred feet from the top. For those without the equipment and/or climbing experience this is a relatively fast and easy way up one of the most beautiful high peaks in the High Sierra.

Approach: Follow the approach on pages 92-93 to the Whitney-Russell Col. From there walk easily down and across to Mt. Russell's south face aiming for the obvious J-shaped arete (the Fishhook Arete).

The Climb: From the base of this arete follow talus slopes up and right until you reach a short (80-foot) headwall. Climb up and left up a chimney ramp system (Class 3) to the summit ridge. Take special note of where you hit the summit ridge so you can easily find it on the way down. Go left along the crest to the summit. The view of Mt. Whitney across the way and pretty much everywhere else on the horizon makes every huff and puff worth it.

Mt. Russell

East Arete ~ Class 3

First Ascent: Norman Clyde, June 24, 1926
Approach Mileage and Elevation Gain: 5.0 miles–1.0 mile on good trail, 3.5 miles on mostly good cross-country. 0.5 mile on steep, slidey talus. 5,200 feet of gain.
Total Gain: 5,800 feet
Area Map: Page 94
Photo: Page 108-109, 114 as descent route

This classic arete is one of the finest Class 3 routes in the High Sierra. First climbed by Norman Clyde on one of his many solo trips, it must have been a daunting sight when he viewed it from the route's beginning at the Russell-Carillon Col. It still is, but now at least, one approaches it with the knowledge that it's much easier than it first appears.

The Approach: See pages 91-93 (The North Fork Approach)

The Climb: Simply follow the arete for roughly half a mile over the east summit to the higher west summit. Turn all difficulties on the right (north) side of the ridge where ledges and ramps provide easier going.

The Descent: Retrace your steps.

Chapter Eight

Up the East Face

The Story of the First Ascent, Mt. Whitney's East Face
by Norman Clyde
from the book *Close Ups of the High Sierra*

Among mountaineers, second in fascination to the making of first ascents is the finding of new routes up mountains already climbed, especially if these are difficult. As opportunities of accomplishing the former gradually diminish, climbers turn their attention to the discovery of new and more arduous ways of obtaining summits of mountains. Walking or riding being a rather tame mode of reaching them, in their estimations, they are forever seeking new problems of ascent which they may match their skill and strength, puny as these may be, compared with the forces of lofty mountains.

Scalable with comparative ease from the south, west and north, Mt. Whitney, the highest peak in the United States, has lured mountaineers in the quest of a "real climb." Last season a fairly difficult one was found going from the east up a broad chute culminating in a notch on an arete running northward from the peak and giving access to the north face which was followed to the summit. Unsatisfied with the discovery, however they began to consider whether the apparent sheer east face of Mt. Whitney might not be scaled.

The great mountaineer, Norman Clyde PHOTO: Bancroft Library

It was with this object in view that a party of five motored westward from Lone Pine toward the base of the Sierra Nevada during the forenoon of August 15 of the present year. The group was one of proven climbing ability. It consisted of Dr. Underhill of Harvard University, one of the most expert rock climbers in the United States; Francis Farquhar of San Francisco, prominent in the activities of the Sierra Club; Jules Eichorn from the same city and Glen Dawson from Los Angeles, both youths, but very skillful in rockclimbing; and the writer of this sketch. It is pertinent too, that the first descent of the new route was made by three Los Angeles youths: Walter Brem, Richard Jones and Glen Dawson, on September 6, 1931.

Having arrived at the end of the road, some eight miles west of Lone Pine, we transferred our baggage from automobiles to the backs of several mules. After a short trudge up the sun-steeped eastern slope of the range we swung around a shoulder and entered the refreshing coolness and shade of Lone Pine Canyon with the summit of Mt. Whitney looking from its head a few miles directly to the west. Charmed by the alluring seclusion of the gorge with floor shaded by pine and fir; with brook resounding through a canopy of birch and willow, with walls of mellow-hued and pleasingly sculpted granite, we leisurely followed the trail to Hunter's Flat, a distance of about four miles, and continued up switchbacks to the south of it to an elevation of some 9,000 feet above sea level. There the packs were removed from the mules.

After eating luncheon, we fitted our packs on our backs and, abandoning the trail began to pick our way up the North Fork of Lone Pine Creek. Within a few hundred feet we came upon a projecting buttress around which we swung, and began to scramble over broken rocks in the direction of a crevice leading up a steeply-shelving granite slope to a ledge running along the south wall of the gorge. Occasionally we stopped to regale ourselves in the luscious wild currants which grew abundantly among the chaotic talus through which we were passing. Below as the stream bounded along sonorously, hidden from view by a dense growth of birch and maple.

Upon arriving at the foot of the crevice, we scrambled up it as best we could, laden with heavy and bulky packs, to a ledge which we followed around a projection. Although the ledge shelved down to a cliff, we strode rapidly along it in our rubber soled shoes, pausing now and then to look down to the floor of the canyon several hundred feet below us, or turning about to gaze eastward through its U-shaped opening and across the wide basin of Owens Valley to the Inyo Mountains—richly colored, glowing in the afternoon sunshine, and with a mass of snowy-white cumulus clouds hovering above them. A scattering of limber pines grew along the lower portion of the shelf and as it gradually ascended, considerable numbers of the foxtail variety began to appear. To our left, a vertical wall of granite rose in places to a height of several hundred feet.

Having reached the upper end of the shelf, we crossed a strip of talus to the border of a glacially-formed basin in which grew a beautiful grove of foxtail pines. Through these we filed along to the margin of a meadow at an altitude of some 10,000 feet. It was a fascinating spot, by craggy peaks and to the west of the great pinnacles and steep walls of Mt. Whitney. Being without a trail and difficult of access, seldom has human foot trodden its secluded recess, although but a few miles from Owens Valley. Presently, the sun sank behind the serrated peaks of Mt. Whitney, suffusing a few clouds that wreathed about their summits, with vivid-hued light.

The ensuing dawn was literally "rosy-fingered," the peaks of Mt. Whitney and those on either side of the cirques glowing in roseate light of marvelous beauty. After a hasty breakfast, we were soon on our way northward across the meadow hoary with frost, to the base of a slope which we ascended to a cleft in the rock up which we scrambled to an apron-like slope of glaciated granite. Across this we picked our way along a series of cracks to a grove of foxtail pine in another basin.

With this behind us, we clambered up the point of a long promontory extending eastward from a shallow basin directly to the east of

Mt. Whitney. Along its narrow crest, we sped nimbly to the margin of the upper basin when we halted for a few minutes in order to survey the face of Mt. Whitney, but being able to make little of it, we walked northwestward a few hundred feet to a small lake which afforded a more satisfactory view. After careful scrutiny, a possible route was discovered. At best, however, it would be obviously a difficult one and any one of a number of apparent "gaps" in it might render it impracticable.

Up a steep acclivity sufficiently broken to permit easy progress we steadily climbed to the notch and there were roped up. Dr. Underhill and Glen Dawson were on one rope; Jules Eichorn and myself on the other. The first rope preceded along the shelf, but as feared, it suddenly terminated in a sheer wall. Upon hearing this, the second rope began to scale the face of the gendarme, but this proving rather hazardous, we swung to the right and succeeded in finding a narrow shelf, or rather the edge of an upright rock slab with a crevice behind it, along which we made our way to a notch behind the pinnacle. From this, we descended a few feet, rounded a protruding buttress on narrow ledges, and began to ascend a chute, rather steep but with surface sufficiently roughened to afford good footing.

After an ascent of a few hundred feet we entered an alcove-like recess where further direct advance was barred by a perpendicular wall. There we awaited rope number one which presently arrived and after a short pause climbed over a low ridge into another chimney, rope number two following. Both ropes then clambered up an overhang to a platform. From this, however, progress upward could be made only by climbing a steep and rather precarious crack. Rather than run the risk of a fall we decided to attempt a traverse around a buttress to the left to a slabby chimney beyond it.

As I swung out over the wall below the platform, an apparently firm rock gave way beneath my foot and went crashing down the sheer cliffs directly below, but as no one was in its path and my handholds were good, no harm resulted.

Rope number one then went around the buttress to reconnoiter and after a pause of some time, the other followed. The traverse proved to be one requiring considerable steadiness, as these ledges were narrow and there was a thousand feet of nothing below them. As we came around the projection we were confronted by a gap in a ledge with a narrow platform about eight feet below. There was the alternative of stepping across it—as far as a man of medium height could possibly reach, availing himself of rather poor handholds—or dropping down to the platform and climbing the other side of the gap. Some of the members of the party chose one method; some the other.

Once over the break in the ledge, we were obliged to pull ourselves over a rounded rock by clinging to a diagonal crack with our hands while our feet momentarily swung out over the thousand-foot precipice. We attacked a precipitous, slabby wall availing ourselves of narrow ledges for hand and footholds. A few rods of this, however, brought us to a rounded shoulder with a broad couloir above it.

After halting a short time for luncheon, we proceeded up the chimney, zigzagging back and forth as we clambered over and around great granite steps until we were confronted at the upper end of the chimney by a vertical wall about thirty feet in height. At one side of it, however, there was a narrow crevice up which one might scramble. After removing our rucksacks, we squirmed and corkscrewed up it, the last man tying the knapsacks to the rope carried by the first.

Above the couloir, somewhat to our surprise, we encountered rather easy climbing. We therefore unroped and began to ascend to the right toward the summit of Mt. Whitney. Within a few minutes we came within sight of a cairn a little more than two hundred feet above us.

Quickening the speed, we clambered hastily upward, arriving at the summit, considerably elated by the successful accomplishment of the first ascent of Mt. Whitney up its apparently unscalable eastern face. Francis Farquhar, having ascended the mountain by another route, was there to meet us.

1937 USGS topographic map of the Mt. Whitney area   MAP: Private Collection

After spending an hour or more on the top of Mt. Whitney, the party separated, three following the trail southward in order to ascend Mt. Muir, while Dr. Underhill and myself proceeded to descend the north face to a notch a few hundred feet below the summit. It was an easy descent along a rocky rib and down a wide chute to the right of it.

After an evening spent consuming enormous quantities of food and lounging about a campfire, we retired to our sleeping bags under nearby foxtail pines solemnly silent beneath a sky spangled with innumerable stars over-arching the mountains that loomed darkly around the basin. On the following morning we made up our packs and proceeded down the canyon, pleased at having added another outstanding climb to the already discovered number in the Sierra Nevada.

Bibliography

Brewer, William H., *Up and Down California in 1860-1864*, Edited by Francis Farquhar, University of California Press, Berkeley, CA 1966

Brown, Vinson, *The Sierra Nevadan Wildlife Region*, Naturegraph, Co., San Martin, CA 1954

Clyde, Norman, *Close Ups of the High Sierra*, Spotted Dog Press, Inc. 1998

Croft, Peter, *The Good, The Great And The Awesome*, Maximus Press, Bishop CA 2002

Farquhar, Francis, *History of the Sierra Nevada*, University of California Press in collaboration with Sierra Club, Berkeley, CA 1966

Fiero, Bill, *Geology of the Great Basin*, The University of Nevada Press, Reno, NV, 1986

Friends of the Eastern California Museum, *Mountains to the Desert, Selected Inyo Readings*, Eastern California Museum, Independence, CA 1988

Jones, Chris, *Climbing North America*, University of California Press, Berkeley, CA 1976

King, Clarence, *Mountaineering in the Sierra Nevada*, University of Nebraska Press, Lincoln NE 1970

Knopf, Adolph, *A Geological Reconnaissance of the Inyo Range and the Eastern Slope of the Southern Sierra*, Government Printing Office, Washington, D.C. 1918

Matthes, Francois E., *Sequoia National Park* – A Geological Album, University of California Press, Berkeley, CA 1956

Munz, Philip and Keck, David, *A California Flora*, University of California Press, Berkeley, CA 1959

Norris, Robert N. and Webb, Robert W., *Geology of California*, John Wiley & Sons, NY 1976

Schoenherr, Alan A., *A Natural History of California*, University of California Press, Berkeley, CA 1992

Selters, Andy, *Ways to the Sky*, American Alpine Club Press, CO 2004

Smith, Genny (Schumacher), *Deepest Valley*, William Kaufmann Inc., Los Altos, CA 1972

Starr Jr., Walter, *Guide to the John Muir Trail and the High Sierra Region*, Sierra Club, San Francisco, CA 1974

Storer, Tracy I. and Usinger, Robert L., *Sierra Nevada Natural History*, University of California Press, Berkeley, CA 1973

Whitney, J.D., Geology, Volume 1, *Geological Survey of California*, Caxton Press, Philadelphia, PA 1865

Voge, Hervey, editor, *A Climber's Guide to the High Sierra*, Sierra Club, San Francisco, CA 1962

Zdon, Andy, *Desert Summits: A Climbing and Hiking Guide to California and Southern Nevada,* Spotted Dog Press, Bishop, CA 2000

Index

Peter Croft

Peter Croft grew up on the west coast of Canada on Vancouver Island. As a child he hiked and camped with his families, developing his love of the

outdoors. Since then Croft was drawn to the mountains, wherever he could find them.

Over the last thirty years he climbed from Alaska to Mexico, from Norway through Europe to the Greek islands in the Mediterranean Sea. He dodged aggressive kangaroos at Mount Arapiles in Australia; has secretly hiked Kauai's famously rugged Napali Coast when high

PHOTO: Galen Rowell

surf–the most colossal mountains of water he had ever seen, closed all access; has made trips to the Karakorum and the Himalaya, seeing firsthand the tallest mountains on earth. The Sierra Nevada with its good weather, beautiful trails, lush meadows and firm granite has enchanted Peter Croft like no other place in the world.

Considered one of the leading alpinists today, Croft spent many years climbing Yosemite's big walls and is most famous for his fast-paced one-day traverses of entire mountain ranges. He has appeared in numerous films. In 1991 he was awarded the prestigious American Alpine Club Underhill Award for outstanding achievement in mountaineering.

Croft lives with his wife Karine and dog, Peewee, in Bishop, California right on the doorstep of the High Sierra. Even that doesn't seem close enough.

Wynne Benti

Though she spends most of her time fact-checking in front of a MAC, *Wynne Benti*, has hiked to the summits of more than 600 peaks in California, the southwest and Mexico including El Picacho del Diablo, the highpoint of Baja. A graduate of the University of California, Davis, Benti, who lived in Malindi, Kenya and Copenhagen, Denmark, moved to Bishop a decade ago. She considers the Eastern Sierra one of the most beautiful and ecologically diverse places in the world.